Friends with Everyone

Friendship ...within the Love of Christ

Meg Bucher

Revised Edition, May, 2019.

Brianne and Lauren,

This book is dedicated to you.

God has taught me the most about who I am and who He is through being your mom. I love you both fiercely and compassionately, as Christ loves me. His love for you will never falter or fade, and it's the joy of my life to lead you to His feet.
Tune into His voice above all others. He has a special purpose for and plan for your lives.
You will always be forgiven before you apologize, loved more than you can comprehend, and we will always be 'The Three Musketeers.'

Father,
Praise You for Brianne and Lauren. They are beautiful and wonderful daughters' of Yours. Thank You for letting me lead them to You as their mom. Bless them with Your sustaining joy. Keep them physically safe, and guard their hearts, today and always. May they always know they have a true friend in Jesus, and allow their blindingly bright light to shine huge.

In Jesus' Name,

Amen.

Table of Contents

Section One: How Does God Define Friendship?

Section Two: God's Pursuit of Our Friendship

Section Three: Forming and Fostering Healthy Friendships

Section Four: But What Happens When...

Introduction

We often find ourselves unsettled by loneliness, even when surrounded by people. Why is it so hard to find good friends?

Learning how to be God-guided in our friendships helps maintain His peace in our relationships. When we seek *His* standard of friendship, we begin to discover, and subsequently choose to foster, the meaningful relationships that God litters our lives with. How do we foster long and loyal friendships?

We CAN be friends with everyone, and I think as Christians, we are called to do just that. But we have to adjust our definition of friendship to align with His purpose for it.

Jesus set the bar.
He's not calling us to *be* Him.
He's calling us to be *like* Him.

A step into Jesus' shoes allow us to see how we can love people for Him. What we learn from our walk with Christ allows God to redefine our view of friendship.

What is our purpose on this earth if not to further His Kingdom and spread His love? What is friendship for and purposed to accomplish? Friendship is Jesus' love extended to you through others and through you to others. It's a channel of love. If we categorize and enforce rules upon friendship, we'll forcibly kill it. Romans 7:15 reminds us, ***"I do not understand what I do. for what I want to do I do not do, but what I hate I do." (NIV)***

If we are truly after the pursuit of a holy life and changed heart, friendship can be another way God's kindness blesses us, and furthermore a channel of connection through which we can minister to others.

God is best qualified to pick our friends. Like anything else in life, His purpose is greater than our plan …His will more fulfilling than our agenda.

Jesus didn't turn anyone needing a touch of His friendship away. Throughout these pages we will become familiar with some of His closest friends. Jesus was kind to all, and God worked out the rest. WE should strive for the same, and trust that He will provide friendships and opportunities to befriend.

We will journey through Scripture together, learning how to attain good friendships, maintain the discipline required to be a godly friend to others, and retain God-centered friendships.

Consider the power of your presence in another person's life. Our Father put us on earth together, and there are people that will be placed in our paths purposely. Who will they see? An open-armed greeting, or a shut door?

Jesus was selfless. He made time for people, even the ones that were considered annoying and burdening. He risked it. Being friends with everyone requires a heart guardedly open to anyone. Like His.

In the following chapters, we will look at friendships from three distinct angles, in order to better understand it's purpose and function in our lives. First, we'll try to get a better understanding of how God defines friendship. Then, we'll make sure that we know how earnestly He seeks ours. Finally, we'll discover that there is a way to to form and foster friendships with everyone God places in our paths.

Have we accepted the most important friend request of our lives? Jesus, our Savior, waits with His hand extended, for the day we choose to surrender our lives to Him. He waits specifically for you, who He has always known. Promising never to leave us, He is the only One truly qualified to hold "best friend" status.

Embracing who He says we are allows us to become a better reflection of His love in our lives. Friendship starts in the early hours of the morning, pouring over His Words, and aligning our lives to His purpose in prayer. Full confidence in who He says we are, and Whose we are, allows us to understand His purpose for friendship in our lives.

I'm excited to go on this journey with you! Years and years and years of prayer and pouring over God's Word have gone into this message on friendship. I was long ago dubbed the girl who *"can't wait to be friends with everyone,"* for good reason. For God's reason, each season and lesson in friendship has allowed me to understand His character and my purpose better.

My hope and prayer for each reader is that friendship will take on a new meaning. That we will be better friends with our Best Friend, to ourselves, and to everyone else that witnesses our Love.

Prayer is a huge part of my life, and it's been an enormous part of the process of this message. There will be prayer woven throughout this book, to help us connect to Christ as we seek His meaning for the relationships in our lives.

Raised in a devout Catholic family, I attended Catholic school through the 8th Grade. Prayer was a part of our everyday lives, but as I grew older, I began to see how personal prayer can be. I remember one time, specifically, when I felt the healing power of God through prayer. I went to church to write my uncle's name in the prayer request book, and knelt down in an empty pew to pray for him. I remember doing this often, and it remained habit even after he miraculously pulled through the massive stroke that changed his life forever.

Prayer launches our lives into a more personal relationship with God, based on what He's pulled us through. Evidence He hears our prayers illumines when we glance over our shoulders at His faithfulness.

Friendship is no different. We can trace His tracks in our friendships through heard and answered prayers. Talking to God can feel awkward if you've never prayed that way before. Don't worry! Prayer doesn't have to be hard.

Word associations help when training our minds to adapt to a new process, like establishing change in our prayer lives.

W. -Worship. Praising God for who He is.
R. -Remember. Thank Him.
A. -Ask for forgiveness.
P.- Petition -Storm the gates of Heaven for His help.

WRAP. We take great care to wrap a package for someone who means a great deal to us, as opposed to the last minute dash for the stash of tissue and recycled bags for the birthday party we thought we had a few more days to prep for. No matter what we put into our prayers, God hears us. He sees us and loves us. He's not waiting for us to change, get our act together, memorize prayer, or understand all of the Scriptures. God wants to hear from us right now, as we are. He longs to be a part of our journey. Psalms is full of verses that promise His presence and active participation in our lives. It's a good place to start if words don't come easy to you.

"Worship the Lord with gladness; come before him with joyful songs." Psalm 100:2 NIV

Worship is a simple way to make a grand gesture. God sits above all, yet He has chosen a personal relationship with each of us. To praise Him in prayer is to set the tone by placing Him in His rightful place, above all else in our lives.

"Give thanks in all circumstances; for this is God's will for you in Christ Jesus." 1 Thessalonians 5:18 NIV

Remember to thank God. Gratitude improves our attitude. Paul, author of the above verse, learned to be thankful in the midst of impossibly uncomfortable circumstances. Jail. Shipwreck. Beating …I can't say I'd start singing thanks in any of those situations! But I want to be, so I thank Him. Not only for the things that offer me comfort and blessing in this life, but the purpose behind my trials that I cannot yet see or understand.

"If we confess our sins, he is faithful and just and will forgive us our sins and purify us from all unrighteousness." 1 John 1:9 NIV

Ask for forgiveness. Worry, impatience, laziness, harshness, manipulation, lies, overspending, over …anything… I cannot wait to hand over the list of things I can't handle daily. "I'm sorry" is not a magic eraser. Anyone whose felt the sting of repetitive hurt understands how building blocks of trust can be hard to rebuild once toppled. Yet, as a result of our repentant hearts (repent meaning we are actively trying not to repeat our mistakes) that's what God does.

Imagine knocking the entire Lego Harry Potter castle that just took 'your child' hours of concentration to build off of the kitchen table. It's in shambles. You don't even know where to start or where all the pieces flew to. That's our sin. And in a snap response to a confessed and repentant heart, that castle is back on the table like it never moved. God's forgiveness is unfathomable to us.

"He hears us." 1 John 5:14 NIV

Petition. Storm the gates of Heaven for His help. Lift up your worries to Him. All of them. Ask for healing, guidance, wisdom, and revelation. Deposit prayers like money in a bank account, praying ahead for our children and their futures. Don't be afraid to ask God for the impossible, because He might just hand over a miracle. Don't' be discouraged if prayers aren't answered a certain way, because His way is better. In fact, more than we can ask for or imagine. *(Ephesians 3:20)*

Friendship is something we have to figure out, and prayer will help us get there. Keep the lines of communication wide open as we seek God's guidance down the road of friendship. Let's pray…

Father,

Praise You for these pages, and Your purpose for them. Your creativity is reflected in us, and all that surrounds our daily lives. Help us to stop and notice the scene we are walking through today, and the people You have lovingly placed in our lives.

Thank You for every reader turning the pages of this message on friendship. Thank You for another day to live out our purpose on this earth. Thank You for our friends, both here and gone. For the people that have marked our lives for the better, helped steer us when we strayed, and taught us there is strength and wisdom on the other side of hurt.

We lift up our worries and doubts to You, today. Father, forgive us for pride. Both the kind that begs us to think we have it all figured out, and the kind that threatens to disqualify us. For the hurt we've caused our friends over the years, and any un-forgiveness that threatens to linger in our hearts. Search our hearts, Lord.

As we seek to understand friendship through the lens of Your purpose, open our hearts and minds to absorb the Truth You reveal to us. Scripture says, **"Keep on asking, and you will receive what you ask for. Keep on seeking, and you will find. Keep on knocking, and the door will be open to you."** *(Matthew 7:7 NLT)*

Let our hearts be convicted to change, grow, and befriend. Help us to understand the opportunity we have to be light in dark places, and a life raft to someone's sinking ship. May our hearts be open to receive the friendships through which You pour Your love into our lives. On Your behalf, in Your honor, show us how and send us out into the world to be friends with everyone.

In Jesus' Name,
Amen.

Section One

How Does God Define Friendship?

Chapter 1

Who Does God Say Our Friends Are?

Now that we have set the tone of our mission prayerfully in God's hands, let's dive in to discover how He defines friendship.

The New Shoes

"I can't wait to be friends with everybody!!" I shouted, adding a gleeful heel-kick to my stride.

Doubled over in laughter, my excitement for new teammates to arrive on campus the following day was impossible for my teammate's introverted persona to digest. We ambled down the sidewalk, dodging lopsided cracks in the temporarily quiet college town. The August humidity strung the smell of road-pies left behind by Amish travelers alongside the wafting aroma of fresh baked cookies from a nearby factory.

"Ahhh, the sweet smell of home," I thought as we ran by the *"Home of Nice People"* water tower.

Home away from home, at least. My fully packed pick-up truck, Claudia, had been sitting outside my teammate's apartment all week, waiting for the campus dorms to open.

Blabbing on through every stride of our easy run, I could barely contain my excitement for the upcoming school year.

New people.
New teammates.
New friends.

They would undoubtedly change the dynamic of our team.

I recalled my own nervous entrance, shaking from the tips of my hair to my freshly laced Asics, which soon-after adorned all the dirt from the bottom of Coach's shoe.

"There, now you don't have to worry about getting them dirty...you can just run," he mused as the entire room busted in contiguous laughter.

In every season of life there are people in place. Not every person is active in every season. Not every friend can be everything we need. God's perfect timing most certainly encompasses the friends that adorn our lives.

The common misconception about friendship is that it's *solely* our responsibility to choose our friends. There will be people that come into our lives for reasons other than a God-placed friendship. Tests, trials, and our turn to speak truth. Times to choose "walk away" status based on where our lives are pointed. When we relinquish the control of association to God, who encircles us with what ...and who ...we need, our friendships breathe easier, we find clarity on who the "walk aways" are, and we experience peace in our relationships.

Learning to be God-guided in every decision of our lives requires submission to Him in every area our lives, including our friendships. This frees us from the pressure to solve every conflict and misunderstanding, instead separating actions from people. God promises to defend and speak truth to us, emboldening us to love people unexpectedly.

Who will walk through the door with bright white shoes next season? Who does God say our friends are? They are the people reflecting His love in our lives.

The Biblical Definition of Friendship

Proverbs 17:17 is a commonly referenced verse in regards to friendship. A look into the different layers of this verse helps us better understand God's definition of friendship.

"A friend loves at all times, and a brother is born for adversity."
Proverbs 17:17 (NIV)

"Friend," on the surface of the original Hebrew language it was written in, is a noun meaning *'friend, companion, fellow, another person." (Strongs 7453)* But the origin of that word stems from a Hebrew verb meaning *'to pasture, tend, graze, feed.' (Strongs 7462)* Other definitions of this verb include *'to shepherd, teacher, herdsman, flock, to associate with, be a friend of, to be companions, to be a special friend.'*

God weaves friendship into the way He shepherds us, placing us in each other's paths, and tasking us to take care of each other. A shepherd sticks with his flock. A herder to his cattle. I think God wants us to understand that friendship is more of a charge and a duty, than a convenience or an accessory.

"Love" in Proverbs 17:17 is a primitively rooted Hebrew word that means *'human love for another, for objects (food, drink, sleep, wisdom), for or to God.' (Strongs 157)* The love we have for and to God is built into the fabric of who we are. It's as basic as the need for the physical requirements of our human bodies. Do we realize that the reciprocal love of friendship has an immense effect on our

spiritual health? When we are faced outward, God provides companionship and fellowship through the love of a friend.

Extremities are red flags for untruths and impossible feats.

"Anything with 'always' or 'never' in front of it completely disqualifies your argument," I frequently remind my kids.

Let's think about this verse in that context, and then search our memories to find a friend who has never failed to love us, adverse times and all.

If I'm being completely honest, I'm not that kind of a friend. My human nature is way to selfish to be tuned into any one friend's constant state of peace. There's only One who can stand up under that kind of pressure, and His name is Jesus. The spotless lamb. The Son of God. And our very best friend. Our Proverbs 17:17 friend. *"All times ...adversity."* Do we realize that we should be looking to Him first, before we seek counsel and support from anyone else?

2 Samuel records much of David's friendship with Jonathon. It reflected a loyalty that covered distance and dispute. They weren't able to *Snapchat* across battle lines. Long increments of time went by without communication. Could our modern friendships handle days and months of complete silence?

"No change of outward circumstances should abate our affection for our friends and relatives," Matthew Henry's Commentary states, *"But no friend, except Christ, deserves unlimited confidence."*

The Friend Request

What began as a good laugh on a long run expressed my passion to love and encourage others, but it was my relationship with Jesus that continues to teach me how to be friends with everyone. It's become and infamous laugh that my old college xc teammates and I love to share, and a journey that I am thrilled to cut you in on.

For far too long, my well-intended plight to be friends with everyone was sought through my own solutions, standards, guidelines, and motives. It left unnecessary scars and heartbreak in my wake. When I surrendered the God-planted desire to be friends with everyone back to the Lord, He began to unpack the understanding of my heart's desire to be friends with everyone. Old friendships were restored and renewed, and my heart became better prepared to receive the blessing of new friendships, too.

The most important friend request I ever accepted was Jesus.' I surrendered my life to Him in those dirt-covered running shoes, and He's never left me through all of the triumphs and the trials. He taught me to let others off the hook, not to expect them to fulfill a purpose or a peace in me that only He could. Grounded in my Savior over the last two decades of my life, I have stumbled through the lessons that have led me to write these pages.

There is a verse in the Gospel of John that affirmed the stirring of my heart to stop putting my friendships first. ***"How can you believe if you accept praise from one another, yet make no effort to obtain the praise that comes from the one and only God?" John 5:44 (NIV)***

The NIV Study Bible notes, *"The Jews had their attention firmly fixed on people. Their emphasis on self-seeking and on the human praise showed that they did not accept the one who came from God, and therefore they missed the praise that comes from God."*

I don't want to miss God's praise. Praise from people, and my praise of others, is nothing if not rooted in Christ. All other compliments and encouragement will fall away, fade and fail us. But His Word is Truth. Jesus is Truth. He, who knew us in our mother's womb, compassionately walked this earth to crush the deathly consequences of sin. Love fuels all life. John begins His gospel by reminding us,

"In the beginning was the Word, and the Word was with God, and the Word was God. He was with God in the beginning." John 1:1 (NIV)

Who knows us better than Jesus? Who knew us then and came to earth to feel what we feel? He felt betrayal and criticism, but also loyalty and love. He knows that we cannot perfect a single one of those elements outside of His love. All too often, we find ourselves conflicted over our own imperfections. We bite at each other and shame each other. But that's not Jesus' version of friendship. His is one of love, forgiveness, compassion, loyalty, and steadfastness.

His hand in mine, I began to surrender all of the icky hurts that I had accumulated over the years. With His love came conviction and restoration, redemption and a softened heart. He began to overturn the rocks of my past to reveal the purpose for which He had allowed them to roll into place.

The Family God Says is Our Family

Jonathan surely helped King David in his time of need. He put himself at risk to protect a throne that should have been his to accept after his father, King Saul. Though he stood with his father unto death, Jonathan knew that God intended David to be king.

"Friends love through all kinds of weather, and families stick together in all kinds of trouble." Proverbs 17:17 (MSG)

Talk about being stuck between a rock and hard place. On one hand, Jonathan could have sided with his father, betrayed his friend, ignored God, and assumed the throne. Or, faithfully trusted God and remained loyal to his friend David. Jonathon knew their friendship was much more than a coincidental meeting followed up by common interests.

"'But if my father intends to harm you, may the Lord deal with Johnathan, be it ever so severely, if I do not let you know and send you away in peace. May the Lord be with you as he has been with my father. But show me unfailing kindness from my family- not even when the Lord has cut off every one of David's enemies from the face of the earth.' So Jonathan made a covenant with the house of David, saying, 'May the Lord call David's enemies to account." 1 Samuel 20:13-16

As these two friends pursued obedience to the Lord, their lives, though brought so closely together for a moment in time, would tragically be torn a part. Verse 17 follows the above passage,

"And Jonathan had David reaffirm his oath out of love for him, because he loved him as he loved himself." 1 Samuel 20:17 (NIV)

The Move

It wasn't St. Patrick's Day, but since I was Irish everyone in the class had written something nice to me on cut-out shamrocks put together in a book for me to remember them by. Atop my sleeping bag on the powder blue carpeted floor of my new room, tears streamed down my cheeks as I clutched the heartfelt book of four-leafed clovers.

My best friend's yard had met the back of mine. Memories of laughter in the branches of the old cherry tree flooded down my cheeks as my hand swept over the scar it's trunk left on my knee. Tap dancing on the back deck of the playhouse my daddy built, and drifting over to her pale yellow house instead of mine on the walk back from the bus stop.

There were no frozen sponge iced packs when I got my fingers slammed in the old clunky brown doorway of my new school. The hallways were tan and drab and all of the other girls had known each other since they were in pre-school. But what seemed like an impossible situation to adapt too soon became one of my favorite places on earth.

New friendships breathed new life into my loneliness. Two years later, I walked into a new classroom to begin a new year. *"Bloom Where You're Planted"* was stapled above the chalkboard. God moves us into the light, so that we can bloom. And sometimes He throws a jar of Skittles atop the teachers desk …just because He loves us.

The Friendship Pact

David's lament for Saul and Jonathan is recorded in 1 Samuel 31:19-27. *"How the mighty have fallen!"* he cries. With a heart truly after God's own, David harbored no bitterness towards Saul. Jonathan, though protective of David's whereabouts, fought beside his father and brother, and fell in battle alongside them. *"A friend is always loyal, and a brother is born to help in the time of need." Proverbs 17:17 (NLT)*

It wasn't the first time these two friends would mourn together. After Jonathan's covenant promise to the house of David *(1 Samuel 20:16),* they waited on the Lord's affirmation and direction.

" The day after tomorrow, toward evening, go to the place where you hid when this trouble began, and wait by the stone Ezel. I will shoot three arrows to the side of it, as though I were shooting at a target. Then I will send a boy and say, 'Go, find the arrows.' If I say to him, 'Look, the arrows are on this side of you; bring them here,' then come, because, as surely as the Lord lives, you are safe; there is no danger. But if I say to the boy, 'Look, the arrows are beyond you,' then you must go, because the Lord has sent you away. And about the matter you and I discussed—remember, the Lord is witness between you and me forever." 1 Samuel 18:19-23

Imagine Jonathan's sadness, as the actions of his father proved his intent to kill his friend.

"Saul hurled his spear at him to kill him. Then Jonathan knew that his father intended to kill David." 1 Samual 20:33

Jonathan would continue to warn David *(1Samuel 19:1;42; 23:8),* but the two would part ways. When the boy picked up the arrow and returned it to his master *(1 Samuel 20:39),* David knew he was being hunted by a crazed king.

"After the boy had gone, David got up from the sound side of the stone and bowed down before Jonathan three times, with his face to the ground. Then they kissed each other and wept together- but David wept the most. Jonathan said to David, "God in peace, for we have sworn friendship with each other in the name of theLord, saying, 'The Lord is witness between you and me, and between your descendants and my descendants forever. Then David left, and Jonathan went back to town." 1 Samuel 20: 41-41

David would now walk out the rest of his life without his friend by his side.

The Perspective

God-placed memories bring us back to what He's brought us through, in order that we may apply it to the current status of our hearts. God shelters our hearts from hurts we can't see coming. How often do we weep over loss that might have been a blessing? My 8-year old broken heart sobbing on the pale blue carpet was in God's protective hand. Because that's who He is.

Some painful seasons undoubtably make us stronger and wiser in our faith if we'll allow God's hand to move the pieces into place. The Truth about who God is assures us that He makes good of all things.

There's something so special about the perspective of motherhood. I made a vow to protect the entity of friendship in my life, so that my daughter would be equipped to do the same in hers. By honoring God with our lives, and seeking a relationship with Him daily through His Word, we can confidently trust His movement in our lives.

Perspective comes with onset of applied wisdom. The application of wisdom, at any age, is accomplished through God's living and active Word at work in our lives, transforming us from now until the day He calls us home to heaven.

"Whoever does not love does not know God, because God is love."
1 John 4:8 (NIV)

We crave Love. Not just the fleeting feeling of liking dark chocolate and coffee so much we can barely start the day without it, or loving another person so much we fear the day we might have to live on this earth without them.

The seeds that God has planted along the path of our lives are watered with His Word. Our obedience to His commands allows us to bloom into the purpose that He has uniquely designed for our lives. When we pursue God's Word like that, we get to know His character, and *"God is love,"* takes on a fresh new meaning around every season He pulls us out of and grows us through. To be a good friend, and to have good friends, we need to have a relationship with the one true Friend. The One who will never leave us, always hear us, defend us, and love us …even confront and convict us …more than we will ever be able to understand this side of heaven.

So what does God say about friendship, and what can we glean from the Bible on how to be a good friend? How do we know what to reasonably expect and hold friends accountable for; and when is it healthy to forgive and forget? How do we aim to be friends with everyone God places in our path to befriend, God's way?

Through the indwelling of the Holy Spirit in every Christ follower, we can do the humanly impossible. With discipline, we can let insults roll off our backs, and make smart choices when they fly out of one mouth repetitively. By replacing our thought tracks with God's truths, we can love who He made us to be. We can, with God's strength and Jesus' example, be friends with everybody. But it's not realistic to expect it to come easily, or be executed perfectly this side of heaven. We can love Jesus a lot …but we are not Him.

The Bible Besties

Long after the passing of his friend, David honored his friend Jonathan, and the covenant his friend had initiated.

"Is there anyone still left on the house of Saul whom I can show kindness for Jonathan's sake?" 2 Samuel 9:1 (NIV)

In accordance to the portion of their covenant, *"and do not ever cut off your kindness from my family—not even when the Lord has cut off every one of David's enemies from the face of the earth" (1Samuel 20:15)*, David learned of Jonathan's son. Lame in both feet, David took him in.

"Don't be afraid," David assured Mephibosheth in *2 Samuel 9:7, "for I will surely show you kindness for the sake of your father Jonathan. I will restore you all the land that belonged to your grandfather Saul, and you will always eat at my table."*

Love elevates friendship past our self-centered default.

"A friend loves at all times, and is born, as is a brother, for adversity." Proverbs 17:17 (AMP)

Other languages have many different words for love. This kind of love is clearly one of those contexts that we who speak English miss out on. The same word we use for our "love" of McDonald's fresh fries, our *"love"* of the Browns *(a different kind of love only Clevelanders understand)*, the shirt we *"love,"* and the spouse we *"love."*

The love that David had for his friend, Johnathan, was a sacrificial love. *(Dictionary of Bible Themes 8298). 1 Thessalonians 2:8* mentions this same type of love, ***"Because we loved you so much, we were delighted to share with you not only the gospel of God but our lives as well."*** The NIV Cultural Backgrounds Study Bible says that "Greeks considered dying for someone the greatest expression of love; Paul had actually risked his life among them."

David knew that he must choose his friends carefully. In the ancient times that they lived in, it my be advantageous for a family member to get rid of another relative. Jonathan, who's father was chasing David, illustrated the importance of faith in God's purpose over human loyalty. Although he remained loyal to his father, he helped David escape.

God's purpose for friendship in our lives doesn't always look like a social media friend-aversary montage. But if we are willing to seek Him first, we will undoubtably run into others who are doing the same thing. Do we trust God enough to let Him redefine the meaning of friendship in our lives?

"A true friend loves regardless of the situation, and a real brother exists to share the tough times." Proverbs 17:17 (VOICE)

To find out who God says our friends are, we need to seek more of God.

Let's Pray…

Father,

We give you praise for the Words of wisdoms that You have brought to our attention today. How great You are, for making sure we are not alone. Thank You for teaching us to value our relationship with You above all others on this earth. Thank You for the example that Jesus set for us in how to love our friends and be good friends. Scripture says, "A friend loves at all times, and a brother is born for adversity." (Proverbs 17:17 NIV)

Through the story of David and Jonathan's friendship, You show us a great example of the loyal love we are to aim for and look to receive in our lives. "And Jonathan had David reaffirm his oath out of love for him, because he loved him as he loved himself." 1 Samuel 20:17 (NIV)

But, moreover, Father, You have given us the example of Your Son, Jesus. "In the beginning was the Word, and the Word was with God, and the Word was God. He was with God in the beginning." John 1:1 NIV Our true and constant friend, who has promised never to leave us. Help us to love with a heart like His. Grow us to understand and obey the conviction of 1 John 4:8, "Whoever does not love does not know God, because God is love."

Paul and other early church leaders understood the power of Christ's love. "Because we loved you so much, we were delighted to share with you not only the gospel of God but our lives as well." 1 Thessalonians 2:8 Bless our hearts to understand how to love others as You do. As we seek friendship in this world, help us to face outward in service, as extensions of Your love.

Father, You promise to provide for us. You are our provider. We know that You will fulfill our every need, including friendship and companionship, when we follow You with all of our hearts. Outward facing, servant minded, and trusting You with the details. "A friend is always loyal, and a brother is born to help in the time of need."

Proverbs 17:17 (NLT) Help us to recall, remember, and understand this verse as we embark on this journey to learn how You define friendship.

In Jesus' Name,
Amen.

Chapter 2

Why Do We Need Friends?

"As the Father has loved me, so have I loved you. Now remain in my love." John 15:9 (NIV)

We need friends in order to remain in God's love, because He has carefully crafted and purposed each life to make an appearance in another's as the extending arms of His love. There is one dictionary definition of friendship that stood out to me more than all of the others in my study:

"Friendship- A person attached to another by feeling of affection or personal regard." - dictionary.com

The love we have for our friends begins with the love He has for us. When we attach ourselves to the vine of Life, love flows through everything we do and to everyone we meet.

As I look back over every friendship that I've mangled, choked, and stomped out in the first four decades of my life, it's a wonder I have any left to claim. But in each season of relational struggle, my focus wasn't on His love, but my friendship. Or, my status as a friend, and what that was supposed to do for me.

"Friend- Verb. To add (a person) to one's list of contacts on a social media website. n. A person associated with another as a contact on a social media website."

People can only affect our hearts to the extent to which we allow them permission. We can simply "unfollow" people who aggravate us on social media, but in the real world of friendship, we are called to obey God's Word and will for our lives …and our friendships. Scripture says to *"take captive every thought,"* which surely encompasses those we dedicate to friendship. I don't believe friendship is a snap decision simply based on the people in proximity to us, but I do believe there is a window of time where we should prayerfully consider the reason for their presence in our lives.

We need friendship for encouragement, accountability, and company. His banner over us is love, and it ripples through daily life in the company He keeps within reach. We do need our people. We need friends.

The Friendship Fog

***"I have loved you as the Father has loved Me. Abide in My love."
John 15:9 (VOICE)***

The fog cast an eerie lure of anxiety over a familiar place one February day as I swam down the small-town city pier through a cloud of fog, searching wide-eyed for the lighthouse I knew was there. I checked my footprints to make sure I was still on the pavement and not the glazed-over River, and gazed upwards and all around for any shred of light peaking through. The wispy top layer of fresh snow revealed one single set of down and back footprints to the right of mine.

I released my dance moves to the new album I couldn't stop listening to, and took full liberty of the backstage curtain of fog to praise my

God anonymously as I trekked out to the lighthouse that was still assuredly out there beyond the mist.

In my quest to "be me," I occasionally feel akin to my walk down the pier in the fog. I lose sight of what I know is there; and what I know isn't there, I want to see. God always has a way of breaking through the thickness with a shard of light. Many times, that glint of hope comes in the form of a friend.

It's been two decades since my high school friend passed on to heaven, yet I still can't bring myself to attend a class reunion. Knowing she won't be there solidifies the fact that lasting female friendships are hard to come by. God has a way of placing people to speak truth into our lives. No one could expose my terrible choices, applaud the successes I was too timid to share, or shake up a Sunday service by clapping and dancing in worship with me like my friend did. For a chronically insecure girl like me, her loss was devastating.

Through the long road of healing, God has graciously bloomed flowers of remarkable friendship. Each God-placed friend has extended the love of Jesus to me when I have needed it most, sometimes unknown even to them. When we seek God with all of our hearts, He blesses us with people to share life with. [1]

Jesus sweetly assured His closest friends, and us as well, that change can produce a "flourishing vineyard." We tend to clutch onto our friends and resist change. Can you image how firmly the disciples wanted to hold on to Jesus?

"At a time when all of His disciples are feeling as if they are about to be uprooted, Jesus sketches a picture of this new life as a flourishing vineyard—a labyrinth of vines and strong branches

---

[1] "Finding the Power of Female Friendships Where I Least Expected." **https://www.crosswalk.com/faith/women/finding-the-power-of-female-friendships-where-i-least-expected.html**

steeped in rich soil, abundant grapes hanging from their vines ripening in the sun.

Jesus sculpts a new garden of Eden in their imaginations—one that is bustling with fruit, sustenance, and satisfying aromas. This is the Kingdom life. It is all about connection, sustenance, and beauty. But within this promise of life is the warning that people must be in Christ or they will not experience these blessings." -VOICE commentary on John 15:9

Jesus assures them *"a flourishing vineyard,"* awaits. New friendship can be scary. Letting distance grow between current friendships is scary. A new home, job, or mission is scary. But God promises to surround us with support. Jesus flipped their imaginations around to focus on the possibilities that lie beyond their fear of letting go, and describes "a new garden …all about connection, sustenance, and beauty."

The paraphrase of these verses brought Christ's Truth to the front of friendships. We can trust His placement of friends in our lives, because He is trustworthy.

This book about friendship has been spinning around in my head for many years. Perhaps, it began circulating because I could never quite find a book to address all of the hangups and mess-ups in my trademark quest to "be friends with everyone."

I believe God put this message in my heart to convict it to change. He is teaching me, growing me, and has pulled me through some of the toughest relational lessons I've ever been through during the process of getting these words out of my mind and into my Mac. I have been hurt by people. I have hurt people. And through it all, God has shown me a little bit more about the human capacity to love, and be loved. Friendship is important, because it's important to God. Whether our place is to step back, or move in, we have a friendly obligation to everyone He places in our path. Yep, even the ones we'd like to seal ourselves off from, and the ones who won't let us in. Everyone.

The Start

"I have loved you just as the Father has loved Me; remain in My love [and do not doubt My love for you]." John 15:9 AMP

Making a new friend, or approaching a new season with an established one, takes a slow walk in humility. John 15:9 instructs us to *"remain in His love,"* and snap judgements and circles of gossip definitely lie outside of that love.

The Greek word for *"love"* in John 15:9 is *"agape."* The NIV Study Bible states that agape and the verb form agape occur only 8 times in the first twelve chapters of the Gospel of John, but 31 times in following four chapters. During that time, Jesus was in the upper room with His disciples, for the Last Supper, and then on the road to Gethsemane.

The last words of *THE FRIEND* to His friends were about love.

"You do not realize now what I am doing, but later you will understand." John 13:7 (NIV)

Jesus washed the feet of his friends. He not only spoke of love, but gave them so many examples of how to love each other. He loved them by serving them.

Do we stoop low to serve our friends? To love our friends? The peace that we forfeit is a result of a self-centered view of the purpose and function of friendship. Jesus was outwardly focused, not worried about who would pay Him back or be there for Him when He was lonely …He trusted God first.

Why do we need friends? It's not the other people in our lives that we need, but the lesson in trusting God that we learn through them. We so desperately need to soften our hearts from the hard battering they take from humanity's self-centered default.

"Very truly I tell you, one of you is going to betray me." John 13:21 (NIV)

I remember walking in on a juicy conversation that starred me as the topic of gossip one afternoon. On the way to a friends house as a favor, it's the last thing I had expected. Even though I had been hurt by this friend in the past, I kept forgiving and returning. Each time hurt more than the last. Every betrayal of trust burned my eyes and lumped my throat all but shut.

NIV Cultural Backgrounds Study Bible states that typically someone who was betrayed was said to be a bad judge of character. Jesus knew He would be betrayed, proving His wisdom, but I don't believe it hurt Him any less knowing ahead of time.

God, Himself, hurts for us. He is concerned for us. Jesus' compassion, the same that drove Him to trod the ground we do all the way to the cross, led Him to feel the suffering betrayal of a friend, and the complete denial of another.

"Will you really lay down your life for me? Very truly I tell you, before the rooster crows, you will disown me three times!" John 13:38 (NIV)

Peter wept when that rooster crowed. Judas eventually took his own life after betraying Jesus. Jesus taught us the most important lesson of all through these two friendships. Immediate forgiveness, and compassion for our friends beyond what we understand.

We can learn to walk in prayerful consideration of another soul by taking aim at Jesus' example; learning to immediately submit our situations to Him in repentance before the bitter roots of pride shoot up.

How to be a Loyal Friend

Loyalty. Defined as faithful to one's sovereign, government, or state; but also faithful to one's oath, commitments, or obligations. [2] In our relationship with Christ, loyalty is seeking daily to follow Him. To be a loyal friend, we can look to His example on earth, but we can't pull it off here on earth. However, it is possible to be a loyal friend by choosing to be there when we say we will be …and we're needed. We would be wise not to keep setting aside time for those who consistently dishonor ours. Friends will be there before they are asked and when they say they will be, if even to sit in silence or leave a note of encouragement on the doorstep.

"A friend is always loyal, and a brother is born to help in time of need." Proverbs 17:17 (NLT)

Divorce is an ugly word that no one dreams of putting onto the list of events that describe their life. But that's was what I was faced with.

"Do you want me to go with you?" my friend asked.

I immediately said yes, and we sat side by side in the waiting room as I waited to be called in to sign the papers. My heart caught in my throat each time the elevator opened. Alone, I faced the new label that I would carry for the rest of my life. My friend had been through it too, and shared some of the common threads of heartbreak that wove through our stories.

"The goal in our female relationships should be to encourage one another's security. Not enable one another's insecurity." Beth Moore, So Long, Insecurity

---

2 **dictionary.com**

My friendship with her to this day is a side-by-side story of redemption, as we both not only put our lives back together and have watched some incredible blessings unfold in our lives. We share something not many women share, and I'm forever grateful for it. It's not easy to walk out of a wake of destruction, let alone to turn and encourage others that have suffered through the same. I didn't expect to find a friend that would sit by my side that day, but I'm forever grateful for her. Jesus promises never to leave us, and sometimes He places a friend by our side to remind us. [3]

Jesus is a Loyal Friend ...and a Great Running Partner.
"I've loved you the way my Father has loved me. Make yourselves at home in my love. If you keep my commands, you'll remain intimately at home in my love. That's what I've done- kept my Father's commands and made myself at home in his love." John 15:9-10 (Message)

Comparing the trace of my tracks in the snow, one set revealed a wispy on the tail of my heal where I had drug my feet. The other set, after I noticed and corrected the problem, was nice and clean. Dragging feet cause runners overuse injuries from this mark of improper form.

In my friendships, I'm challenged to peer into the past before I bite back.

"There is power in friendship. If it didn't matter, threatening to end it wouldn't be our knee-jerk reaction." Anna Rendell, The Gift of Friendship.

We don't have to fear forgiveness. The asking or receiving of it. **You may open the door of relief for someone who needs to unload the**

---

[3] "Finding the Power of Female Friendships," **crosswalk.com**

burden of imperfections that they carry, too. We all carry them. *"We all fall short." Romans 3:23*

Jesus was "at home" in His Father's love. When He stepped back, it was to be alone with His Father in prayer. We tend to turn on our heals and run when relationships start to implode. Judas ran. Peter ran and wept. Yet, we can picture the gaze that Jesus points at him as that bird crowed one more time …it wasn't an accusatory gaze. It was an "I love you, anyway," promise.

"I am the true vine, and my Father is the gardener. He cuts off every branch in me that bears no fruit, while every branch that does bear fruit he prunes so that it will be even more fruitful." John 15:1-2

Every branch, of every one of us. Like the Master Gardener that He is, our Father blooms us in beds full of colorful flowers. Mingling and mixing, and complementing each other. We fight the same choke and clutter of the same weeds, yet when watered stand tall together. Some of the flowers sway in the wind beside us in one season, are gone the next. Some keep coming back. Some remain constant regardless of the season or passing of time.

The Mexican Sunflowers that I plant in my yard each year have become the talk of my neighborhood. The first year I planted them, I had no idea how tall they would grow, let alone that they would attract hundreds upon hundreds of Monarch butterflies. This past summer, I planted them in the same place, and not one grew back. The butterflies flitted around my yard in the fall, but slowly stopped coming, with no where safe and protected to land.

I don't know why those flowers didn't bloom that season. We surely missed cutting fresh blooms and scattering them around the house in pretty vases. Friendship stays well-watered when attached to the vine. Unlike my flowers, the people that come and go from our lives are not coincidental. Some are God-placed to rescue us and others to stretch us, but the Master Gardener will prune all of us slightly through each of our friendships.

"You are already clean because of the word I have spoken to you. Remain in me, as I also remain in you. No branch can bear fruit by itself; it must remain in the vine. Neither can you bear fruit unless you remain in me." John 15: 3-4 (NIV)

Our faithful Father directs the symphony of friendship in perfect time.

The Friend that Tracked Me Down

"Orphah kissed her mother-in law goodbye, but Ruth clung to her." Ruth 1:14

She had invited me to Fellowship of Christian Athletes, which ignited my faith and led to my official surrender to Christ. Her life reflects her solid faith. Even amid the pressures of college life that all but took me out, she remained steady in her faith. When I became a ghost, she never stopped looking for me. Before social media was a thing, it was possible to disappear for a little bit. That's exactly what I did as my life unraveled and I destroyed the shattered remnants of my first marriage. I started to pull back and disappear, ashamed and scared that God would never be able to use me, and my past friends would never forgive me. But this friend never gave up trying to find me. Jesus never gives upon us.

"God sees over our lives by teaching us what His Word says. He also surrounds us with people who can speak truth to us and by showing us He can work through every circumstance if we'll trust Him. But see, if I stop reading His Word, God can't teach me what it says. And when I isolate myself from others who love God, I can't be poured into. Or, if I am determined to make things happen my own way, I might miss what God has for me." Nicki Koziarz, 5Habits of a Woman Who Doesn't Quit

"I've been looking for you!"

The message popped up on my screen as I dove into the world of social media. Reconnected and faith rekindled, she helped me remember who I was, and that no season of darkness could take me out unless I let it. I had hurt everyone around me. Flaky, and inconsistent. Who wanted a friend like that? She saw past the struggle to who I was, and I will never be the same because of it. She clung to me like Ruth did to Naomi! Her faithfulness sparked a revival in my soul. Through her friendship, Jesus tapped me on the shoulder, assuring me that it was silly for me to count myself out … he surely hadn't. [4]

If my friend had focused on the hurt I had caused her, she might not have sought after me. Instead, she choose to remember me for the friend God said I was to her, not the one my mistakes framed me to be. We have an active free will to choose, and to consult our Father in every decision that we make. Will it always lead to a reconciled friendship? Probably not. There have been plenty of other friendships that have faded into black. But for the one chance to have a friendship like this one, it's worth taking every notion to God in prayer, and seeking wisdom in His Word for direction and purpose.

"When someone smacks you, the instant and unavoidable response is to turn away from them. The've forced you to do so. But what you do after that moment changes everything." Holly Gerth, The Gift of Friendship

---

4 "Finding the Power of Female Friendships Where I Least Expected." **https://www.crosswalk.com/faith/women/finding-the-power-of-female-friendships-where-i-least-expected.html**

She changed the fate of our friendship that day, and we've since made an effort …reciprocally …to trust that God has great plans for our friendship and our lives.

The Change

"Just as the Father has loved me, I have also loved you; remain in my love." John 15:9 NET

I picked up a cross necklace a few years back when I needed constant visual reminder that Jesus was with me no matter how tight the drama in my life was wound. The first time I put it on, I noticed there was inscription on the back. *"Be the change."* As a new coach implementing lots of changes, I took it as a sign that I was running in pace with God's plan. Really, it just meant to be me through the change. A me that was changing …the growing kind of change.

"I am the vine; you are the branches. If you remain in me and I in you, you will bear much fruit; apart from me you can do nothing." John 15:5 (NIV)

That necklace reminded me to stay attached to the vine at all times. When we walk into new assignments, we are never alone. We have a friend in Jesus, who promises never to leave us, and He can proclaim peace over any situation when we draft off of Him. But when faced with challenge, doubt, worry and fear will attempt to seep in through any crack we allow them to. Our clutch on the vine becomes weakened, and before we know it we're lying flat on our faces wondering what happened.

"If you do not remain in me, you are like a branch that is thrown away and withers; such branches are picked up, thrown into the fire an burned." John 15:6 (NIV)

That wasn't an easy season for me, in so many ways. Struggling to balance a team, a family, a disease, and a departure, I needed friends. I needed branches. I needed extensions of His love …stat.

One friendship, and then another, time piled more unrest atop my toiling. Because when we depend on our friends to save us from sinking, the water rises faster than we can swim. But Jesus will always have His hand outstretched, hoping we'll grasp it before our last gaping breath.

"If you remain in me and my words remain in you, ask whatever you wish, and it will be done for you. This is to my Father's glory, that you bear much fruit, showing yourselves to be my disciples." John 15: 7-8 (NIV)

There was nothing else to do but fall into the vine and let it rehydrate my spinning and sad mind. Crying out to God in pain and heartbreak, I felt Him there that day. The simple assurance of His presence was instantly calming.

Christ's compassionate kindness means everything to someone who's everything is crumbling.

I was diagnosed with AS, a disease in which the spine begins to fuse. X-rays from world-renown hospitals had solidified the future treatment and stature of the rest of my life. Sometimes we forget that Jesus has the authority on this earth. And sometimes He miraculously reminds us. He did me, a few short weeks after that good cry, with the disappearance of that incurable disease.

I was happy just to know I wasn't alone. Just to know that He was there. But His heart is moved with compassion and concern for us. That is the true miracle. He truly has more in store for us that we can ask for or imagine.

When my kids come to me annoyed with a classmate, the sting of my own experience of un-acceptance flares back to the surface."There's always something good you can find about a person," I teach them, "Find it, and focus on that." Kindness can mean everything to someone. Focus on the Light beyond the fog.

I believe friends populate our lives because we were never created to walk life's lessons alone.

"We need someone to look us in the eye and say, "You're my favorite."" Dawn Camp, The Gift of Friendship.

Church friends, Bible study friends, high school and college friends, family, bloggers, work peers, neighbors and far away friends, Facebook friends, and authors who write words that resonate so much with our hearts that they feel like friends…

Jesus is the perfect definition of friendship. Because of Him we can go to our Great God in times of need *(Hebrews 4:16),* trusting He's placed enough Light in our lives to pierce through the fog.

The Friend that Reminds Me

"Jonathan made a covenant with David because he loved him as himself." 1Samuel 18:3 (NIV)

We were fast friends, but it would take years to truly understand why God had brought us together. I was a young and inexperienced Cross Country coach, and she had been the first person to call me a leader since I was a kid. That season we shared bumpy bus rides, and cold and muddy Saturday afternoons running around in wellies and losing our voices out of our passion for those runners.

"People care more about what you share with them than what you ever say to them." Ann Voskamp, The Broken Way

I don't think we realized, on all those bumpy bus rides and mud filled courses, that God knew then how much we would need each other now. Little did we know, that both of us were in the midst of trying season's of our lives. Looking back, how I wish I would have listened more to her story, asked more questions and passed out more encouraging notes and hugs. Now that we both know a little bit more about why we became friends in the first place, I try to squeeze into her "what's going on's" whenever I can.

We pursue Christ, together, through a Bible study that we co-lead and a children's ministry that we get excited about. She's teaching me to lead by the way she leads- with humility, diligence, sincere concern, passion, and strong faith. She will pull me out of my mulling and tell me to push on and push through …and I do.

I trust her friendship, not because either of us have it all figured out, but because we know Who does.

Female friendships are hard to find and even harder to foster. Wait patiently. Traverse through life grounded in Christ, studying His Word daily and chasing after His calling on your life. Along the way, He will place unmistakable friendships in your life …sometimes where we least expect it. [5]

When we remain in His love, we can give more our of our hearts than humanly possible to our friends; and receive that same peace and love in return.

The Friend Room

"I have loved you just as My Father has loved Me. Stay in My love." John 15:9 NLV

---

[5] "Finding the Power of Female Friendships Where I Least Expected It." **https://www.crosswalk.com/faith/women/finding-the-power-of-female-friendships-where-i-least-expected.html**

I love how this version uses the word, "stay." It's an easier word to comprehend in some ways than, "remain." Remain suggests to wait on, or wait for; while stay simply means to stay put. Sometimes, we need friends to help us stay put while God reveals why.

Friend-"n. A person who gives assistance; patron; supporter."

By that definition, it would seem that everyone we become acquainted with, whether through the local PTO or Twitter, would fall in the 'friend' room. But God says, we are to abide in His love at all times, trusting He will place friends in our path.

"Friend-n."a person who is on good terms with another; a person who is not hostile."

Although it would be more convenient to ghost friends that disappoint or fail us, we must first take into consideration why we've crossed paths. When we're the subject of gossip and our friend is the one spewing it, we'd rather run than sit and stay in that friendship. The people we befriend are supposed to be our friends. We expect them to be loyal, and we hope that they'll agree and align with us.

But that's not the sole purpose of friendship. Not Biblically. It would be easier, but Christ never promised us easy. He promised us love. He commanded us to love. And then He littered our paths with people *to* love. People that are hard to love, but worth loving. Friends. Whom we can't expect to be perfect, but need all the same. Because they are extension of His loving encouragement, guidance, compassion, kindness, and disciplinary love.

Jesus called us to love each other, in the only way He knows we're capable of love. In an imperfect, messy, Christ dependent way.

An old college teammate of mine used to categorize friends.

"Megan, Megan, Megan..." he so coyly explained while we all laughed over his analogy, *"you're nooootttt quite in the friend room yet..."*

A torturous statement for a young college girl who just wanted to be friends with everyone!

"The friend room is inside the house and up the stairs," and as we all pictured this house, I couldn't stop thinking about how to earn my friend status.

"You're almost to close enough to knock on the front door ..."

Still makes me laugh to this day, and I can picture my best friend laughing with me in shock that he would be so bold as to say that! His philosophy was smart in premise, to guard his heart, but hidden under my love to laugh at a great bit, was my hurt to discover I wasn't good enough to qualify.

What we deserve in this life is far more than we can ever earn. Jesus died for all of us, equally, because He loves all of us, equally. And we, like He, need a heart that is open to the possibility of being friends with everyone if we want to be friends with anyone.

"Friend-n. A member of the same nation, party, etc."

The key to attaining and retaining friends is to seek God's will in the situation. We have to define what that is in order to seek it. And to determine whether the next step of a friendship is worth developing, it must be put through some prayer tests. It takes a healthy pursuit of God to grow and maintain friendships.

There are some friendships in the Bible that illuminate the kind of friend I want to have ...and I want to be. Naomi and Ruth, Jonathan and David, and Paul and Timothy. As we go on this journey of friendship together, we'll learn together from God's Word and their stories, how to make friends, keep friends, and grow friendships.

Attain, retain, and maintain.

The Letters

"As the Father has loved me, so have I loved you. Abide in my love." John 15:9 (ESV)

In seeking His definitive standards for friendship, God laid a relief upon my heart in that I will never seek out a better friend to me on this earth than the best friend He's already given me.

His name is Jesus.

"Be a leader," echoes in my ears. A piece of advice from a wise Abbot I had the privilege of be-friending as a Catholic Elementary School girl. But lead what? And who? That answer is still unraveling.

Following Jesus is hard, and my twenties would take me farther away from Him than I would have every dreamed possible in my church-going, Jesus-filled childhood.

He has slowly put the pieces back together, blessing me beyond my wildest imagination. Over a decade of marriage and two wonderful daughters. But the by-product of un-qualification that past missteps leave behind can paralyze my sense of purpose. Could God still use me?

One such day, I stumbled upon the letters. Written when I was thirteen, for spirit day. Leading up to the Catholic Sacrament of Confirmation, every 8th grader spent a day away from family, reflecting on the next step in faith we were all about to take. Those letters encouraged me then, and reminded me of who I am.

We are under the assumption that we change over time. And though God slowly sanctifies us until the day we arrive in heaven, we are the same soul He has always loved with abandon.

The first letter was from my Dad, reminding me of the great relationship we had, and asking me to let him help me through the tumultuous times that teenage life would assuredly bring upon me.

My mom's letter, told me of how much she loved me and would always be there for me, regardless of the little spats we got into. "You're one step closer," she closed her letter with. Everything we go through can bring us one step closer …to Him.

The last letter was from my Grams. She was my sponsor, and the person I could talk to when I couldn't talk to anyone else. She reminded me of how I came to stay with her after Grandpa died, keeping her company, cleaning her house and making her meals. Her love poured out on those pages, assuring me my parents were good, and not to fear going to them with anything. "Keep your standards high, as you do now," she reminded. And at that, my mascara streaked down my face.

I had not kept high standards. I knew better. I love God. I know Jesus. I know the power of prayer and of the Holy Spirit. I read my Bible. But still made bad choices. Horrible choices. Choices far beyond what I ever thought I would be capable of choosing.

But God says it's never too late, and in that moment of soul cleansing, He was reminding me that I was still that thirteen year old girl. My love for Him, nor His for me, has weakened in the slightest. Even through all the heartache and horrible missteps. It was another piece moved back into place. And along the way, the friends He moved into my life helped me move through that tough season to remember and embrace again who He created me to be.

There's never been a day for me that I didn't believe Jesus was there. Can't remember one. The blessing layered in that sentiment alone is enough to leave me tear stained and breathless. We made friends easily.

The Road.

The sun started to come up over the lake, and as I strode along the shoreline in exchange for a seat in church that Sunday, I can't ever remember feeling closer to God. Training for a marathon had been the hardest thing I'd ever done, and that last 20-miler was the greatest run of my life. Every stride felt easy, every hill was a rolling adventure. This was it. The last step in my training before race-day. The farthest I would have to go until I raced for 26.

Months before, in so much pain that the bottom of my feet hurt, I could not imagine coming this far. Being this restored.

I had been diagnosed with a chronic immune disease that caused the spine to fuse, and rushed into treatment to keep it from spreading. At the same time, my parents relocated from down the street to the other side of the country. I resigned from my head coaching position for the local cross country team. My new normal made it dangerous for me to be around sick kids, and my sore back kept me from picking my kids up. After a while, the pain of it all landed me on in a bawling heap on my bedroom floor.

I cried out to God in the ugliest way one can possibly cry. In a way I didn't know I could cry.

A year later, the power of God's hand on my life to hear me and heal me was the most personal display of love I've ever experienced. An X-ray clear of fusion. No sign of disease. A literal miracle.

The first thing I wanted to do was run a marathon so people could see what He did. There had been may teary-eyed moments of triumph coupled with goo stops and frozen eye-lashes. He had run right beside me, every stride.

"Beep."

As I silenced my watch and ended my run, I felt my foot pop. The next day, my chronic achilles injury had swollen to a size of a quarter. All of my training ...all of my goals ...suddenly fell a part. I scrambled to fix and patch and ice, but finally gave in.

I pulled out of the race. But in some ways, I knew I had already won. *"It's not for everyone to see,"* I kept feeling pressed upon my heart, *"it's for you. This was for you."*

Friendship in this life doesn't get more personal than Jesus' love for each of us. No one will ever be our Jesus. He is the only One who can save us like that. But we can try to take the love we receive and pass a piece of it on to a friend.

Whether you've known Jesus for years, or would like to welcome Him into your life for the first time right now, let's take a moment and praise Him for His friendship, and thank Him for our friends.

Let's Pray ...

Father,

*Praise You for Jesus. In John 13:7, Jesus told His disciples, **"You do not realize now what I am doing, but later you will understand."** His sacrifice on the cross gives us direct access to You and Your Word. He came down to earth out of compassion for us, choosing to forgive us for our sins long before our own feet met the earth. As we seek Your purpose and definition of friendship, help us to remember Jesus' words, **"As the Father has loved me, so have I loved you. Now remain in my love." John 15:9 NIV***

Love surpasses our understanding, yet is the most important commandment we are called to keep. It is only in abiding in Love, that we can love others. For Jesus said, **"I am the true vine, and my Father is the gardener. He cuts off every branch in me that bears no fruit, while every branch that does bear fruit he prunes so that it will be even more fruitful." John 15:1-2** Thank You for Him, and for the Holy Spirit that dwells in us when we claim Him as our Savior.

Jesus, we believe in You, and don't want to navigate this life without You. Help us to abide in the Vine, as You spoke to Your disciples. **"If you do not remain in me, you are like a branch that is thrown away and withers; such branches are picked up, thrown into the fire an burned." John 15:6** Take our hand, and stride with us side by side as we dedicate our lives to following You. Take up residence in our hearts, filling us with the peace that comes only from Your presence. We hold tight to this Truth: **"I am the vine; you are the branches. If you remain in me and I in you, you will bear much fruit; apart from me you can do nothing." John 15:5 (NIV)**

Bless us with Your friendship, guidance, wisdom, and a heart like Yours. Help us to remember the lessons that You taught Peter, restoring him after His denial. **"Will you really lay down your life for me? Very truly I tell you, before the rooster crows, you will disown me three times!" John 13:38 (NIV)** We can all relate to Peter, and all struggle with denial. And **"We all fall short." (Romans 3:23)** Just as surely as Jesus knew Judas would betray Him, so will each of us struggle with the rebellion and sin that is lodged in our hearts as humans. **"Very truly I tell you, one of you is going to betray me." John 13:21 (NIV)**

But with Your help, Jesus, we can learn how to serve the people that You place in our lives with the love and hope that we are called to share with others. **"If you remain in me and my words remain in you, ask whatever you wish, and it will be done for you. This is to** *my Father's glory, that you bear much fruit, showing yourselves to be my disciples." John 15: 7-8 (NIV)*

Bless our lives with love, Father. And with godly friends and God-centered friendships. May we be good friends to those who You entrust in our care, showing them the love that You empower our lives with. Holy Spirit, give us more of you. To remind us to focus on Your Word, and help us to remember Your promises. We pray Your will over our friendships, our families, and our lives.

In Jesus' Name,
Amen.

Chapter 3

Friendship's Banner
...What Does Love Have to Do With it?

In order to attain, maintain, and retain friendships, let's look a little
further into God's definition of friendship by peeling off another
layer of Proverbs 17:17 and applying it to what God says about
friendship in our lives.

"A friend loves at all times, and a brother is born for adversity."
Proverbs 17:17 (NIV)

By following the trail of this truth we witness some remarkable
friendships. But first, I think we need to differentiate love and
friendship. Where does one end and the other begin? What is the
difference between a friend and a brother, as eluded to in the verse
above?

The Bible exists in so many translations, and looking at a verse from
different angles can often help us get a birds eye view into exactly
what God is trying to communicate through it.

The New Living Translation says, *"A friend is always loyal, and a
brother is born to help in the time of need."*

The Message paraphrase reads, *"Friends love through all kinds of weather, and families stick together in all kinds of trouble."*

The Amplified Version states, *"A friend loves at all times, and is born, as is a brother, for adversity."*

In contrast to the multiple dictionary definitions for the word, *"friend,"* just one verse of God's Word peered at from four slightly different angles illuminates many different undertones of God's character.

"No change of outward circumstances should abate our affection for our friends and relatives. But no friend, except Christ, deserves unlimited confidence. In Him this text did recline, and still receives it's most glorious fulfillment." - Matthew Henry's Precise Commentary.

Jesus is the only one able to get it right. We can cease striving to hit the nail on the head and start settling in appreciation for the swings we take with our hammers.

"A real friend loves his friend in prosperity and adversity; yea, he is more than a friend in time of need- he is a brother, as affectionate and trusty as one connected by the closest ties of relationship." - Pulpit Commentary.

Who is qualified to be a friend? Loves at all times, is never jealous over status or possessions...who is this person? Jesus Christ is the only one built of such noble character as to ascertain this type of relationship with any person. God has a definite say in it, and if we fight Him on it, like anything else He intends in our lives, there's a really good chance things could get pretty messy. There is no shortcut or once-for-all trick to a good friendship.

The Sissy Patrol

"Sissy patrol is on the roll!" they sang as they skipped merrily down the side-walk…

"Sissies forever …." they tumbled in laughter together as they jumped on their trampoline.

Two years and two months a part, as my little catches up to her big sister …they become more and more inseparable …blessed with a sweet, honest and pure friendship.

I'd like to think their friendship is an answer to the daily prayer I cover their lives with. *"Please bless their lives with godly friends."* It's important. It's life-giving, and it's His love fleshed out in a way I've not witnessed before.

Through all of the sisterly spats that have gone before them and are plentiful to come, I pray that they continue to seek each other out, and seek Him together.

They bond …as we do …over what we have in common. And the One they have in common seems to be the biggest reason they keep coming together. They skip out of church every Sunday, not wanting to leave the family they've formed there, and arm in arm they chant:

"Sissy patrol is on the roll!"

(The plans He must have for those sweet souls.)

The truth is, friend and love have a lot in common. And to be a friend you must know how to love. We learn how to love as we learn who we are in Christ, who is love. When we abide obediently in His love, we can love the friends He litters our lives with.

The Holly and the Ivy

"A true friend is closer than a brother." Proverbs 18:24

Ivy is a climbing vine. Holly is a tree or shrub. I will never hear the "Holly and the Ivy"carol the same way after bearing witness to my two oppositely gifted daughters and their unspeakably close friendship.

David and Jonathan's friendship is highlighted in this verse. There is something that even they knew, comparing it to something even greater than sibling-ship.

I have a strand of ivy living my house that climbs all over the place. She branches off and takes initiative. She is strong and able and uneasily rattled. As she grows up, the vast depth of her giant heart for Jesus and others is coming into view. I find prayers for others in her desk drawer, and when she says she's going to *do something about it,* that's code for, *"I"m going to pray about it and I know God hears me."* She is the carefree joy that a child of Christ personifies.

My holly tree, on the other hand, put down strong roots fast. She knows who she is and what she loves and where she's going …and she's in absolutely no hurry to get there. We can try to move her along faster or into a different spot where there is more shade or sun ..but there's no moving her. She knows Jesus loves her for who she is right now, and has a purpose for her that she can't derail …so she's in no hurry …I mean NO HURRY …to get anywhere at all … ever. She calls her friends or writes them notes, and takes on the hurt of others that aren't even aware she's looking out for them.

The friendship between sisters is different than other friendships. They don't need to talk about who they are, they just sit alongside each other the way they are. They are so drastically different, yet both love Jesus so much.

They reveal to me how much He loves us all for the way we are. So different. Yet so smashed together for a reason.

We're the holly to someone's ivy, and visa versa. When the different parts of us create conflict, don't run for cover. To a certain extent (and we'll get into this more later in the book), be willing to stick out the hard parts.

We're all created in God's image, with specific purpose. Siblings stuck under the same roof have the opportunity to press through the wonder of their paired existence. For the friendships that we endure through misunderstanding and squabble, distance and time, a similar feeling of sisterly pairing arises. Especially when we can begin to look back with a fresh perspective to see how God reached out and loved us through that person along the way.

The Bossy Cow

Side by side, with our arms up in the air and our souls light under the weight of His presence, we sang praise to the One at the core of our lives …and our friendship. The older I get, the more I realize how rare it is to find a friend to seek Christ with throughout life. Someone who meets my enthusiasm with excitement and encourages me in my faith. We share a thousand "bossy cow" jokes.

Friendship can fleet and fade over the years, but ours seems to grow stronger still with time. We've both been through hard times and trials, and our friendship has been God's way to hug us through some things that no one else could. We became Ashland University Eagle teammates twenty years ago, and we've not stopped laughing for much since then.

I have confidence in our friendship because He brought us together.

"A true friend loves regardless of the situation,
   and a real brother exists to share the tough times." Psalm 17:17
(VOICE)

She was the friend who found and pulled me back to face what wasn't going to disappear after my divorce. We've built so many bridges back to Him …in search of Him …over ice cream.

When she suffered from post-partum depression, we sought Him together through it. Prayed her through and praised her entry back into the light …and full night's sleep …and her first marathon. Through the storms of married life and motherhood that He has pulled us through, and the rock of our joy that He is after every trial …we sang side by side that day. The people God places in our lives are not always blood-related, but they do become our Christian family.

On a road trip to worship in concert, we stopped talking only to worship and sleep. To celebrate our kids being in school all day, we set aside a day to laugh and scream on a bunch of roller coasters. In all of my efforts to be friends with everyone …she has been the friend that has taught me the most about what true friendship is.

They are the people who build us up in Him, so that we can be better people to everyone else.

It's not good to go through life alone, and because she is my friend …I know God has given me someone on this earth that will be my voice of reason. She prayed me through the waves, and will laugh with me eternally.

There are few things greater, and more heart filling and soul soothing, than a God-placed friend. It's the closest thing to Jesus' loyalty and love that we get to feel on this earth.

The Crossfire

"I don't see how one can call themselves a Christian and then have a drink."

So much for sharing a casual drink among friends.

"It's judgmental not to hang out with people just because they drink or swear."

Anyone else feel like a friendship yo-yo at times? Sometimes, I feel like I don't even fit in with church people!

It's not our place to judge anyone, but especially not our duty to lace words into ears that are not ready to hear. Only God can soften hearts. However, 1 Corinthians 5:11 addresses an aspect of Christian friendship that the non-confrontational soul in me wants to scatter and run from.

You can't just go along with this, treating it as acceptable behavior. 1 Corinthians 5:11 (MSG)

It's uncomfortable to check someone else's behavior. Who are we to judge? We certainly don't want our mistakes drug out into the light, so why is it our job to correct our Christian friends? Paul explains it best in the Message translation of today's verse in context with the verses that surround it.

I wrote you in my earlier letter that you shouldn't make yourselves at home among the sexually promiscuous. I didn't mean that you should have nothing at all to do with outsiders of that sort. Or with crooks, whether blue- or white-collar. Or with spiritual phonies, for that matter. You'd have to leave the world entirely to do that! But I am saying that you shouldn't act as if everything is just fine when a friend who claims to be a Christian is promiscuous or crooked, is flip with God or rude to friends, gets drunk or becomes greedy and predatory.
You can't just go along with this, treating it as acceptable behavior.

I'm not responsible for what the outsiders do, but don't we have some responsibility for those within our community of believers?

God decides on the outsiders, but we need to decide when our brothers and sisters are out of line and, if necessary, clean house. 1 Corinthian 5:9-13 (MESSAGE)

It's a lot, and it seems really judgmental and hypocritical on the surface, which is why it's a terrifying thing to stand up for what we believe in. But as the famous saying states …if you don't stand for something, you'll fall for anything. Take these verses into the mirror first, and then to prayer.

God promises to give us the words we need when we need them.

Life isn't always about understanding things, and our perspective sight doesn't always allow us a view as to why God asks certain things of us. But we can trust His intentions are always good.

Proverbs 13:20 says, "Walk with the wise and become wise, for a companion of fools suffers harm."

God's standards should be the fence post of our boundaries.

The Step Back

No replies all morning, I had a sneaking suspicion that we were being ignored. Ditched, even. Every suspicion I'd had was right.

"Be like obedient children as you put aside the desires you used to pursue when you didn't know better." 1 Peter 1:13 This verse is a stark reminder of what to do when we feel worldly pain like my daughter and I did that day. First, start the process of forgiveness. Then, we ask God how to guard the hearts, heal the hurts, and hold us close.

Start that process. Otherwise, the bitter root of pride will latch on and seep in through the cracks in our emotions. Hurt needs to be told what to do. the Bible says to take captive every thought and make it obedient to Christ. For as long as it takes, grab those thoughts and replace them with God's Truth.

Walking with Jesus changes us, but our pace of growth won't align with everyone else's.

There will be times when, no matter how much we want to be friends with everyone ...*and believe me, no one wants that more than me* ...we have to handle conflict and allow our hearts space to heal by God's standards.

What I learned that day, and continue to learn from every reoccurring experience like it, is that rejection won't crush me or kill me. In fact, it brings me closer to Jesus. We will often spend our whole lives looking for someone as dependable and reliable and loving and compassionate as He is. We will never find that person. He is it.

The One that shouldered the cross is the only one capable of cradling our hearts.

So all of the coffee dates unhonored, dinners ditched out of, and unreturned text messages are not in vain. Loving people is never wrong, and neither is forgiveness. But the hurt leaves a little bit of a scar after the wound heals. One to remind us to prayerfully guard our hearts. In transition, take the space to welcome other faces.

Be friends with everyone, but know Who your Friend is.

Before we stretch to understand friendship, we must conquer the mirror's reflection. God created us in His own image, out of love, for a specific purpose. Don't make qualifications to deserve the love that never had to be earned. Insecurity can vomit all over friendships.

Often times we over analyze the facial expressions and tones of other people as derivative of our behavior. Sometimes, our friend is just having a bad day and couldn't answer our text until hours later.

The minute we walk away from the mirror, we start to forget what we look like. Remain in Christ to retain the reflection who He says we are. We need to let ourselves off the hook for imperfection. The same can happen as we get up from the Word and walk out into the world.

We cannot attract loyal friendship without living in God's love.

"Love is patient, love is kind. It does not envy, it does not boast, it is not proud. It does not dishonor others, it is not self-seeking, it is not easily angered, it keeps no record of wrongs. Love does not delight in evil but rejoices with the truth. It always protects, always trusts, always hopes, always perseveres." 1 Corinthians 13:4-7 (NIV)

Jesus is love, healing our insecurities and restoring our hearts. When we understand that we can only find that peaceful filling in Him, it allows us to let other people off the hook. We can then begin to see friendship through the perspective eyes of our Savior. He came to serve us, and when we are focused on what God wants us to do and how He wants us to be there for others, He promises never to leave us alone, to defend us, hear us, and place people in our lives to love on us for Him, too.

Let's Pray ...

Father, Praise You for sisters. Thank You for giving us friends within our families. Forgive us when we mistreat each other, as family often does, and bless us to seek You together, always. Praise You for family friendships, and the lessons that we learn from observing them. Thank you for placing us in our families so purposefully, and forgive us for taking that for granted. Bless our hearts with the love we need to reach out to family members.

__Proverbs 18:24__ says __"A true friend is closer than a brother."__ Thank you for revealing the rich truth of this verse. Help us to retain what we've learned about how you define friendship, and the renewed perspective of the friendships in our lives. Praise You for the friends You place in our lives.

Bless our friendships to honor You always, and our lives to reflect Your Son ...our King ...Jesus. Praise You for godly friendship. For the pocket of purposeful encouragement You place in our lives within our church families and mentors in faith. We are reminded constantly throughout Scripture to be lights to the world, but not to be of the world. ***You can't just go along with this, treating it as acceptable behavior. 1 Corinthians 5:11 (MSG)***

Thank You for the friendships we are blessed with in this life where we don't have to worry about being judged for who we are in You. Forgive us for judging others, and for not standing up for what we believe because of peer pressure. Help us to be strong and firm in our faith. For __Proverbs 13:20 says, "Walk with the wise and become wise, for a companion of fools suffers harm."__ And 1Peter 1:13 calls us to action in regards to our perspective on our lives, our callings, and our friendships: " __Be like obedient children as you put aside the desires you used to pursue when you didn't know better."__ Help us to be promptly obedient, and to let the consistent walking out of our faith in daily life be a continuance of our ministry on this earth.
In Jesus' Name,
Amen

Section Two:

God's Pursuit of Our Friendship

Chapter 4

Strong Enough to be a Friend
(Who God Says we are and How He Pursues Us through
Friendship.)

"Taste and see that the Lord is good; blessed is the one who takes refuge in him. Fear the Lord, you his holy people, for those who fear him lack nothing.

The lions may grow week and hungry, but those who seek the Lord lack no good thing. Come, my children, listen to me; I will teach you the fear of the Lord.

Whoever of you loves life and desires to see many good days, keep your tongue from evil and your lips from telling lies. Turn from evil and do good; see peace and pursue it."

-Psalm 34:8-14 (NIV)

Trust in the Lord leads to the right frame of mind. To navigate the reciprocal nature of friendship, our souls must have strong roots of Truth.

"Be strong in the Lord, and mighty in His power." Ephesians 6:10 (NIV)

How do we become strong in the Lord? Strength training. Testing. Pausing the limits of our human capacities, not just physically or mentally …but spiritually. The Greek word for "strong" in this verse is "endunamoo," meaning not just to "be strong, strengthen," but also to "receive strength, be strengthened, increase in strength." (Strongs 1743) Strong faith takes a consistent and disciplined choice to follow Christ, but we must also submit and receive His strength to do and understand what is impossible for us.

The passage that follows Ephesians 6:10 is often titled "The Armor of God." In verses 11-19, through the apostle Paul's inspired words, God shows us how to be strong:

"Put on the full armor of God, so that you can take your stand against the devil's schemes. For our struggle is not against flesh and blood, but against the rulers, agains the authorities, agains the powers of this dark world and against the spiritual forces of evil in the heavenly realms. Therefore put on the full armor of God, so that when the day of even comes, you may be able to stand your ground, and after you have done everything, to stand. Stand firm then, with the belt of truth buckled around your waist, with the breastplate of righteousness in place, and with your feet fitted with the readiness that comes from the gospel of peace. In addition to all this, take up the shield of faith, with which you can extinguish all the flaming arrows of the evil one. Take the helmet of salvation and the sword of the Spirit, which is the word of God.

And pray in the Spirit on all occasions with all kinds of prayers and requests. With this in mind, be alert and always keep on praying for all the Lord's people. Pray also for me, that whenever I speak, words may be given me so that I will fearlessly make known the mystery of the gospel, for which I am an ambassador in chains. Pray that I may declare it fearlessly, as I should." -Ephesians 6: 11-20 (NIV)

The more we pursue God, the more we learn about His character. The result is strength. When we realize just how much He pursues us, our friendship with Him begins to precede any other. Aligned the right way, we become strong enough and free enough to be a good friend, and accept good friendship.

The voice outside the door was pretty routine. I had tried to steal a moment away to go to the bathroom, and fooled myself into thinking that shutting the door would signal the little people in the house to allow me a moment of privacy. *(Bah. Ha. Ha.)* God's sense of humor never ceases to amaze me, and the state in which He met me for this moment was right on cue.

The uncharacteristic hesitation in my daughter's voice led me to ask if she was OK. It hadn't been the easiest year, and my heart broke right along with hers. I had been covering her in prayer and God's Truth. That day, my eyes glazed over as she peeked through a crack in that bathroom door to tell me what was weighing on her heart.

" I want to have Jesus in my heart," my daughter whimpered, *"it's just too hard without Him."*

"I need Jesus, Mommy."

I excused myself to "wash my hands" and then witnessed my daughter handing her life over to Christ as we prayed together. It was a marking moment of pure joy, that sent my prayer life into overdrive on a completely new level. A heart surrendered to Jesus will most certainly face trials and challenges, and strength is what I pray for my girl as she faces the start of the next decade in-step with her Savior.

The Strength to be Joyful

"I have told you this so that my joy may be in you and that your joy many be complete." John 15:11 (NIV)

His strength enables my feet to keep trekking on. *"Be joyful always,"* (*1 Thessalonians 5:16),* is a lot easier to live out when things are sunny-side up. But when life becomes painful, hard, and unfair …lonely and badgered with doubt …it takes **His** strength to keep hiking through the snowy woods.

The Greek word for *"joy"* in *John 15:11* is *"chara,"* (Strongs 5479) which means *"joy, gladness."* But underneath a part of the definition that says, *"the cause or occasion of joy,"* it's defined a little further as, *"of person's who are one's joy."*

When Jesus is our joy, it is complete. His joy becomes ours. He becomes our joy. The root word of chara is *"chairo, "* (Strongs 5463) a primary Greek word that expands the meaning unto *"to be well, thrive."* **The strength to *find* Joy comes *from* Him.**

The Strength to Surrender

The source of our strength isn't something that we can grip, it's a surrender to a source that flows through us.

Surrender means to yield the possession of power, to give oneself up, relinquish, abandon, or *"to give oneself up to some influence, course, or emotion."* Jesus told his disciples, **"Greater love has no one than this, to lay down his life for his friends." John 15:13 (NIV)**

"The branch must remain open to the flow of the vine's life. If the branch were simply wound around the vine tightly, it would still die without producing any fruit." Beth Moore, Portraits of Devotion, Day 216.

On whose accord do we lay down our lives for our friends if we have not surrendered our own into His hands? Surrendering our self-centered disposition for a Christ-centered perspective takes Holy

Spirit strength. A daily, soul-surrendering strengthening, from the vine.

The Strength to Obey

"If you obey my commands, you will remain in my love, just as I have obeyed my Father's commands and remain in His love."
John 15:10 (NIV)

Uninterrupted obedience is unattainable this side of heaven. Even before the constant clamor of criticism that bombards us through social streams, internal doubt has always threatened to disqualify us from the full and vibrant life Christ died to give us.

The same little voice that peeked into the bathroom weeks earlier, recently discovered that discipline remained a part of a Christ-committed life. Frustrated by her own disobedience, that sweet child asked me if He was even in her heart.

"Of course He is," I reassured her, pointing to her heart, *"He will never leave you."*

Christianity is a slow change, an individual walk. Yet, we compare our obedience to those around us and entertain benchmarks that may not be realistic for the current way-point of our hearts. Each day that we choose to walk with Jesus, we get a little stronger. The indwelling of the Holy Spirit provides us with the strength to obediently follow Him.

The Strength to be Imperfect

Lucky for me I grew up in the 90's, or my struggle with perfectionism would have been glaringly obvious. Don't mistake my life for a suffered one …I'm the same high energy crack-up that I've always been. I just don't own a scale. God convicted me of that negative thought cycle long ago, and I choose to obediently stop it.

We will never lack strength to accomplish His will in our lives, when we abide in the Vine.

How easily our hearts can be led down a road full of absolute crap.

"It's a lesson, not your life-story," I assure my daughters when they make mistakes. *"Everyone struggles with difficult choices."*

How can we let our soul's find their worth in a grade, paycheck, weight, good review, re-tweet, or accolade? The strength to be imperfect comes from Christ. If we hold onto anything else but His validation, then we set ourselves up for a good crushing when the external feedback we receive inevitably fails us.

"There is no fear in love," 1 John 4:18a says. Guilt and shame over the mistakes we have made in our lives does not come from God. Romans 3:10 states, **"There is no one righteous, not even one."** Jesus died so that we could live life to the full (John 10:10b). He never said we had to be perfect.

The Strength to Construct Healthy Boundaries

"My goal is that they may be encouraged in heart and united in love, so that they may have the full riches of complete understanding, in order that they may know the mystery of God, namely, Christ, in whom are hiding all the treasures of wisdom and knowledge."

Colossians 2:2-3 (NIV)

Paul was writing to the Colossians in combat of heresy (any belief or theory that is strongly at variance with established beliefs, customs, etc.). The NIV Study Bible lists examples of ceremonialism, asceticism, worship of (or with) angels, devaluing the person and work of Christ, secret knowledge, and reliance on human wisdom and tradition. This was a no-brainer for Paul. He had witnessed

Christ. There were no gray areas for him. He confidently exposed these false practices.

How often do we take a look around our lives and gently rebuke and remove incorrect theology and religious practices? How often do we speak up and speak out about Christ when a world-ism wafts across our eardrums?

Paul was confident! He was strong enough to put up healthy boundaries as to what he was willing to absorb and entertain. We would be smart to focus on Christ the way Paul did.
It takes strength to walk away, kindly disagree, pray for an enemy, forgive an unfairness, process criticism with humility, or forgive ourselves for failure. I once heard this preached by one of the pastors at our church:

"If you want to change, surround yourself with people that get it."

What if God asks us to obediently embrace a season of isolation as we tune into His voice above all others? The Book of 1 Kings tells how God prepared the prophet Elijah. Through my daily journey with First5, I learned that he obediently hid for three years, relying on ravens to bring Him meals twice a day. *"But God wasn't setting Elijah aside — He was setting Elijah apart."* Krista Williams, First5

Strong.

"Be on your guard; stand firm in the faith; be courageous; be strong. Do everything in love." 1 Corinthians 16:13-14 (NIV)

God laid a lesson of strength upon my heart this year, and He continues to teach me how His strength lies behind our joy, surrendering, obedience, imperfection, and construction of healthy boundaries.

"Listen, stay alert, stand tall in the faith, be courageous, and be strong. Let love prevail in your life, words, and actions." 1 Corinthians 16:13-14 (VOICE)

For Love to prevail in our lives, our connection to the Vine must be strong. We can accomplish this by training daily in His Word, and obediently following His lead for our lives.

The Strength to Befriend

Mark and Paul's friendship teaches us never to count someone out as a friend. Mark had proven himself unreliable to Paul. In *Acts 15*, Paul and Barnabas, who had been incredible friends thus far, parted ways over their disagreement about Mark's character. Paul was ready to write him off. But Barnabas saw something in him to be developed. *(Acts 15:39-40)*

Both Paul and Barnabas proved to be right about Mark. Paul, in that Mark was not to come on the mission that caused them to separate. Barnabas saw the potential that eventually developed, and over time Mark joined the group of Christ driven friends.

"Do your best to come to me quickly," Paul said *"Get Mark and bring him with you, because he is helpful to me in my ministry." (2 Timothy 4:5)*

Mark eventually wrote one of the four gospel accounts. Christ never counts us out. Though some friendships are fast and fleeting, they can still have wonderful meaning in our lives, and just might come back around again.

Psalm 119:53 states, "I become furious with the wicked, because they reject your instructions." (NLT)

This verse reminds me so much of the way King David lived his life. David's passionate obedience for God's law proved him to be a rarity of loyal kings in the journey through the 1st and 2nd Book of Kings. In order for David to remain that loyal and faithful to God's law, he said in the NIV version of this verse, *"Indignation grips me..."* The NIV Study Bible Notes explains that *"zeal for God's law awakens the righteous anger against those who reject it and brings abhorrence of all that is contrary to it, but it draws together those who honor it."*

"I am a friend to anyone who fears you- anyone who obeys your commandments." Psalm 119:63 (NLT)

David knew that his strength came from God. And God's strength comes from His Word and our obedience to it. The outside influences we entertain can weary our souls. If we are strength training daily in God's Word, and obedient to His daily purpose for our lives, He will steer us around and through temptation so that it does not derail us completely. When we skip time in His Word, it directly affects our relationships. For David, it would have affected the way he led his country and who he chose to surround himself with. For us, it affects the story we want to tell of our lives, and the purpose we seek God to reveal as it pertains to it.

In David's friendship with Jonathan, we see this character trait played out. In 1 Samuel 18:1, Jonathan speaks of loving David as he loved himself, and the two of them becoming one in spirit. The NIV Notes state, *"It appears that David spoke with Saul at length, and he may have explained his actions as an expression of his faith in the Lord, thus attracting the love and loyalty of Jonathan."*

David's strength of character allows him to decline bitterness at the death of King Saul, and Jonathan's strength of character bode him to die alongside his father in loyalty, despite disagreeing with him. The two were solid in their faith apart from each other.

We cannot serve both God and man. Many kings in the OT tried to make everyone happy, but they were destroyed as a result. Long standing strength, in our relationship with God and each other, comes from the strength obtained from obeying His word. Like Mark and Paul's friendship, sometimes the wisest and strongest move to make relationally is to let go. Part ways. And give God room to move …and strengthen us.

Let's Pray …

Father,

We praise You, for Scripture tells us that we are fearfully and wonderfully made, and that You knew us in our mother's womb. You form us each with individual purpose, meant to further the Gospel message of love and hope through Your Son, our Savior, Jesus Christ. Help us to retain and apply the words of Psalm 34, as we pray them here today:

"Taste and see that the Lord is good; blessed is the one who takes refuge in him. Fear the Lord, you his holy people, for those who fear him lack nothing.

The lions may grow week and hungry, but those who seek the Lord lack no good thing. Come, my children, listen to me; I will teach you the fear of the Lord.

Whoever of you loves life and desires to see many good days, keep your tongue from evil and your lips from telling lies. Turn from evil and do good; seek peace and pursue it."
-Psalm 34:8-14 (NIV)

Father, You are good, and You have good plans for our lives. You pursue us, even when we deny You, and repeatedly sin. In You, we find our hope and peace. It's because of what we know, through our relationship with Jesus Christ, that we can then turn and love others. That takes an obedience that we do not naturally possess. A strength that we cannot build or create in our lives. To experience true joy, we need the abiding love of Christ, who is our Strength and Joy. Love and obedience go hand in hand, as Jesus addresses to His disciples ...and to us. **"If you obey my commands, you will remain in my love, just as I have obeyed my Father's commands and remain in His love." John 15:10**

Allow us to experience the fullness of Christ by searching our hearts for anything that we put above You in the list of priorities in our lives. We naturally want to **"Be joyful always," (1 Thessalonians 5:16),** *but need to abide in the strength of the Vine to experience it.* **"I have told you this so that my joy may be in you and that your joy may be complete." John 15:11 (NIV)**

Forgive us when we fight Your pruning. Oh, how we hold onto the things and the people that we are not ready to let go of. Because we can't see what You see. But You go before us and behind us. You are above us and below us. Forgive our weak hearts, and give us more Love and more of the Holy Spirit to strengthen us in Your Word. For **"greater love has no one than this, to lay down his life for his friends." John 15:13** *We wish to be strong enough to be able to face our lives outward in service to others, with the love that can only flow out of us by abiding in You.*

Remind us that **"there is no fear in love," 1 John 4:18a** *Though the threat of evil and our enemy is real, You are bigger. Bigger than gossip, stirred up conflict, misunderstanding, and broken hearted hurt. Through You, we can choose not to be offended, and we can start the process of forgiveness before bitterness is able to take root.* Romans 3:10 states, **"There is no one righteous, not even one."** *Let our hearts recall this Truth as we look out into the world, so full of hurt and wandering souls. In our efforts to be the best friends we can be, and extending of Jesus' love, and reflections of His grace active in our lives, we pray to keep this verse top of mind and engrained in our hearts:*

"Be on your guard; stand firm in the faith; be courageous; be strong. Do everything in love." 1 Corinthians 16:13-14 (NIV)

In Jesus' Name,
Amen.

Chapter 5

Authenticity
(God's Word is the Authentic Truth.)

"I wait for the Lord, my whole being waits, and in his word I put my hope." Psalm 130:5 (NIV)

Psalm 130:5 was sung on the way to Jerusalem for pilgrim festivals in OT times. The word, "ascents" referring to "steps," referring to the steps of the temple. It's a part of the psalms of 'A song of ascents,' *(NIV Cultural Backgrounds Study Bible)* I was immediately reminded of my journey to a much anticipated worship concert. The preparatory energy I felt on the way evident in high volume of praise music that blared out of my vehicle. Once I arrived, I never sat still, sat down, or stopped singing …praising. It's thrilling to feel God's presence in a packed arena.

In those moments I feel free to let go. In those moments, I feel a piece of home that I wish would never end. And I bottle up as much of it as I can in my memory, blast the music all the way home, and let the momentum of that moment spill out into my daily life. Only the alive and active word of God is equipped to sustain our optimism as we leave experiences like that.

In a pessimistic battleground, we *"wait for the Lord …and in his word put our hope."* He will find a way to keep our spirit overflowing with His goodness if we seek Him with all of our hearts. He will fill our lives with purpose and people if we'll hand over our daily agendas to Him. If we are too busy trying to entertain opinions and activities to save face in society, we will miss out on the hope-laced path of positivity He has laid out for our days. And we will miss the mark of His purpose for friendship in our lives.

In a world where everyone screams loud about living their *"truth,"* we are called to live His. It's not the popular way, the easy way, or the painless way, but it is the most positive way. The most hope-filled way.

We were not meant to walk this world alone. Though each of us carries a purpose and character unique to us, God places others around us be the hopeful embrace of friendship that we need to move forward in opposition. When we are true to who we are in Christ, we find the friends that He knows we need …and those that only He knows …need us.

The Peer

"When I am afraid, I put my trust in you." Psalm 56:3 ESV

King David wrote Psalm 56 when the Philistines captured him in Gath *(Lucado Life Lessons)*.

"Isn't this David, then king of the land? Isn't he the one they sing about in their dances: 'Saul has slain his thousands, and David his tens of thousands?" 2 Samuel 21:11 (NIV)

The strength to live authentically comes from God, alone. King David's encouragement was centered in confidence on the Source of all courage. Living our *full* truth out loud comes from bravely walking within our God-placed purpose. Comparing our lives to those around us, and the mold of societal acceptance, chokes our ability to live uninhibited. But life exposed to the Light sets us free.

The Hidden Heart

When I first earned the freedom to drive, I began to exit the highway early on the way to my family's favorite summer hangout. Windows down and Alanis turned up, I dreamt of what it would be like to swap the suburban hustle for a sleepy lake-town life. Little did I know, roughly fifteen years later, God would move my family onto a piece of land that my '86 Nova passed by hundreds of times.

We unwrapped and repacked Christmas the year that we moved from our beloved starter home. The tree was reassembled and each ornamental reminder was placed back on it's branches. Excited beyond the practicality of installing any window treatments, everyone in that sleepy little lake town saw our life in plain view.

Suddenly the plethora of windows we chose to let the daylight stream in allowed all a glance in when the sun went down. Since our house sits on the only busy road in town ...we immediately ordered blinds!

"When I'm afraid ..."

Charles F. Stanley points out that *"the psalmist does not say, 'if I am afraid,' he says, 'when I am afraid.'"*

David was afraid of Saul. He was on the run, and hoping to be considered insane, so he could continue to run.

"He pretended to be insane in their presence; and while he was in their hands he acted like a madman, making marks on the doors of the gate and letting saliva run down his beard." 1 Samuel 21:12-13 (NIV)

Is this seriously the King David that killed Goliath? Fear is a slippery slope. They bought his act, and he continued to run.

"Look at the man! He is insane!" 2 Samuel 21:14 (NIV)

We all face something in life that makes us want to close all the blinds and hide from the world. God promises never to leave us, and forgive our sins when we confess them. Fear causes us to assume we are alone and unforgivable. Fear propels us to re-confess sin He has already forgiven.

The Labels

In an attempt to stretch farther than I could reach, a vase teetered and came crashing to the ground in pieces. I picked up the pieces, but the tiny shards were too small to be glued back together. It made me think about God's sole ability to piece my slivers together after a battle with fear.

"I put my trust in you."

The MacArthur Study Bible states that *"Confidence in the Lord is a purposeful decision, replacing an emotional reaction to one's circumstances."* David was definitely having an emotional reaction as he ran from King Saul, but he eventually remembered what the Lord had said. God's Truth can snap us out of temporary insanity. Hiding with his men in the back of a cave, King Saul entered to 'relieve himself.' After David snuck up and cut off a piece of Saul's robe, he had an attack of conscience. *(2 Samuel 24: 1-5)*

"The Lord forbid that I should do such a thing to my master, the Lord's anointed, or lay my hand on him; for he is the anointed of the Lord." 2 Samuel 24:6 (NIV)

Labels can be leveling, especially the ones that we are hesitant to claim. There are certain things we don't post on social media, or bring in up in casual conversation, because it's hard to believe they belong to us. We'd rather close the blinds.

The redemptive power of Christ pieces every tiny shard back together. He rolls grace on like a glorious combination of BioFreeze and Gorilla Glue. We don't have to stop living life or hide what we perceive as a lack of progress. The journey back to who He says we've always been is a testimony to His great love. Don't draw the blinds on that.

Charles F. Stanley says in his *Life Principles Bible Notes, "God does not tell us to ignore our anxieties, but to bring them to Him and realize that He can overcome any terror we ever have to face."*

The Roles

My husband and I were too distracted by the beauty of natural light to think about the ramifications of people peering into our lives. Christ did not die for us to live life afraid of exposure.

"I came so that you may have life, and have it to the full," Jesus said in John 10:10 (NIV)

"God, whose word I praise ..."

When Saul was finished relieving himself, David followed him out of that cave. ***"My lord the king!" He bowed as Saul turned around. (1 Samuel 24:8)*** He stepped out from the dark cave and into the light, exposing his truth, and the pieces were put back into place.

"You have treated me well, but I have treated you badly," Saul replied as he wept allowed. 1 Samuel 24:16-17 (NIV)

Living our lives exposed to the light grants us freedom. When we turn up the volume on other voices, opinions, worries, shame, and regret, we become self-focused and selfishly protecting what *we* fear to be unforgivable mistakes and missteps.

Authentically living for Christ begins with a real relationship with Him, in prayer and Scripture. The ultimate friendship in life lies within His redeeming and restoring grace. David walked out of that cave to face Saul, reaffirmed by remembering who God said he was. **Our stories, labels, and lives, exist so that others may experience the love of Christ.**

"When struck by fear, I let go, depending securely upon You alone. In God- whose word I praise- in God I place my trust. I shall not let fear come in, for what can measly men do to me?" Psalm 56:3-4 (VOICE)

Spirit-led truth and honesty expose and improve our authenticity, and our proven loyalty over time comes from the ability to stay aligned with God's Word and attached to the Vine. How often are we confident enough in our friendship with Christ to go out on a limb for our friends, as Jonathan did for David? Too often, we feel stuck in the middle of claiming our authentic and God-given purpose and entertaining questionable chatter. *Gossip. Here-say. Did God really say?*

Chatter hurts. It excludes, it's unfair, and it's cruelty reaches depths beyond we cannot fathom. Christ makes us trustworthy friends. We don't do that by our power or our naturally inclined motives, but by His hand on our lives. By taking the time to breathe in His word, and sit and listen to what He has to say. By obeying and living out what He says, not just nodding with closed eyes and hands up on Sundays. Bottling it up and taking it out into life, embracing another life with those arms, closing those eyes in prayer beside another soul God needs us to sit with. Authenticity.

"No doubt there have to be differences among you to show which of you have God's approval." 1 Corinthians 11:19 (NIV)

We stand out because we worship the One and only authentic God. The devil wants us to play right into his hands, hating each other and becoming more divided by the day. Despising denominations and differences in opinion …in appearance. All unique, we stand out synonymously to and for our Father. His church, moving in all different parts and patterns, but together for the hope of the Gospel.

"When you come together, it is not the Lord's Supper you eat, for what you are eating, some of you go ahead with your own private suppers. As a result, one person remains hungry and another gets drunk." 1 Corinthians 11:20-21 (NIV)

Everyone is invited to the Lord's table.
God loves every one of us for who we are, and where we're at. Authenticity begs us to go out into the world open to God's adventurous plan for our lives. When we pray to the Holy Spirit for the wisdom to authentically love others, I believe He is faithful to show us the way. Jesus said Himself, there is nothing more important than loving one another.

Let's Pray …

Father,

There is only one authentic source of truth …You and Your Word. We celebrate the Scripture we get to learn from and communicate with You through. Thanks to the sacrifice Jesus made with His life on the cross, we get to communicate with You, and through Your Holy Spirit in us, listen to Your counsel concerning our everyday lives. "I wait for the Lord, my whole being waits, and in his word I put my hope." Psalm 130:5 (NIV) We pray for the strength to reflect the love You pour into our lives daily through Your Word, Father.

With a solid foundation of Scripture, and close relationship with our Savior, Jesus, we can trust Your purpose for every relationship in our lives. We are promised to face troubling and hurtful times in this life, and our friendships are no exclusion. We are all imperfect, and that's a hotbed for a good emotional mess from time to time. Fear can overwhelm our ability to make good decisions by the people we've been entrusted with. But when we face the Saul's in our lives, we can hold tight to David's wise words, **"when I am afraid, I put my trust in you." Psalm 56:3 ESV**

Jesus did not come so that we would fear the King Saul's in our lives. There will be many instances where we are either aimed at or misunderstood, but Jesus reminds us, **"I came so that you may have life, and have it to the full," Jesus said in John 10:10** *A full life is one surrendered to Christ. The One who has the ability to save us from unjust situations, and defend us when we cry out for mercy. Forgive us for faltering in our fear, and failing to stand firm in our faith under pressured moments. It's scary sometimes. In moments when we feel attacked and alone, help us to remember this truth:*

"When struck by fear, I let go, depending securely upon You alone. In God- whose word I praise- in God I place my trust. I shall not let fear come in, for what can measly men do to me?" Psalm 56:3-4 (VOICE)

From the variety of trouble, fear, and struggle with sin that David experienced in his life, we can know assuredly that our lives will carry no less. A man after God's own heart, David still lived a human life. Jesus promises that we will have trouble in this life, but to take heart, because He has overcome the world. That's one major piece of God's eternal plan that David didn't have going for him. We do. We live in New Testament times.

Knowing how much Jesus loves us, and that we don't have to pay the eternal penalty that we deserve for our sins, should allow us to extend grace to everyone we come face to face with ... but that does not come easily for us. When we struggle with forgiveness and battle with fear, help us to live that boldly in our faith. For when we authentically run to You, we can trust that You will provide all that we need.

Bless us with authentic, lived-out, faith in Christ.

In Jesus' Name,
Amen.

Chapter 6: Mission Minded

God-placed Friends Along the Way

"Moreover, at Daniel's request the king appointed Shadrach, Meshach, and Abednego administrators over the province of Babylon, while Daniel himself remained at the royal court." Daniel 2:49 (NIV)

Just 27 verses earlier ….

"He reveals deep and hidden things; he knows what lies in the darkness, and light dwells with him." -Daniel 2:22

One of my favorite coffee mugs has the Eiffel Tower on it, because I dream of taking my daughters there someday.

"Merci….thank you."

"Bonjour …hello!" I sometimes practice my French while waiting to pick them up from school, harboring the dream of crepes, castles and coffee …

New translation births the dream of possibility in our hearts.

One afternoon I arrived home with the miraculous, disease and fusion-free x-ray results, and a new lease on life, I saw this verse stuck to my mirror:

He reveals deep and hidden things; He knows what lies in the darkness, and light dwells within Him. Daniel 2:22

He could see what I couldn't all along. He had everything under control. I choose to hold my dreams in the same regard, now, practicing French before understanding how we will get there. Knowing that some dreams will remain wild and untamed, but others will come true beyond the realm of human possibility.

Our dreams remain blurry until He brings them into focus. In His time. By His Grace.

Christianity gives birth to the possibility of the dreams in our hearts. Jesus shines light into the cracks of our hearts and the corners of our minds that we didn't even know were dark.

Dreams are dark to start, until He reaches in and tells us what they are all about …shows us what they mean. Little by little, as we seek Him in His Word and follow behind His steps, He shows us who we are, and why He placed those dreams. Every once in a while, He blesses us unexpectedly. That's Love. That's Grace. That's God.

The Blinders

"Deep refers to something inaccessible. What is in the darkness is hidden from sight." NKJV Study Bible.

God goes before us and behind us, above and below us, and surrounds us with His love. We may think of provision as physical or tangible things, but God also knows who we will need in certain seasons of our lives. Friends can serve as shards of His light. And not always to comfort or console us. Sometimes we need to be gently pulled from the fire about to scorch our socks. Only a true and trusted friend has the ability to cut through the noise we so easily let ourselves become distracted with.

Daniel was able to see to it that his friends, Shadrach, Meshach, and Abednego, had a place in the government. Even in the darkness, under the reign of a pagan king, shards of light remained. In Daniel Chapter 3, the three friends are thrown into the fire for refusing to bow down and worship anything but the one true God.

"King Nebuchadnezzar, we do not need to defend ourselves before you in this matter. If we are thrown into the blazing furnace, the God we serve is able to deliver us from it, and he will deliver us from Your Majesty's hand." Daniel 3:16b-17 (NIV)

They were thrown in, and then emerged from, the fire.

"He said, "Look! I see four men walking around in the fire, unbound and unharmed, and the fourth looks like a son of the gods."

Nebuchadnezzar then approached the opening of the blazing furnace and shouted, "Shadrach, Meshach and Abednego, servants of the Most High God, come out! Come here!"

So Shadrach, Meshach and Abednego came out of the fire, and the satraps, prefects, governors and royal advisers crowded around them.

They saw that the fire had not harmed their bodies, nor was a hair of their heads singed; their robes were not scorched, and there was no smell of fire on them."

Daniel 3:25-27 (NIV)

Bright burning flames temporarily blind us, and standing too close, let alone right in the middle of it, burns us. Daniel was not afraid to take his position in the royal court, nor were his friends to take up their government appointments. None bowed down or caved in to the culture around them. The powerful proximity of friendship has the ability to strengthen us in high pressure situations.

These men were confident in the task at hand. They had unshakeable faith in God, not each other. The three friends weren't expecting Daniel to jump into the fire with them. I doubt they were expecting anyone to jump in. They just leaned into their faith in the one true God, knowing that in the end, that was the authentic and right thing to do. A healthy dose of fear can fuel good friendship.

Many scholars say Jesus met them in the fire. Undoubtably, it was a God-ordained miracle. These friends had their heads on straight. They're not mentioned in the Bible after the furnace. Daniel, who's position most likely had him busied with other duties, was not there to defend his friends.

I doubt they were mad at Daniel for putting them in that position, or for neglecting to be there on their behalf as their lives were at stake. We all need sticky friends like that.

The same trickery used to throw the three friends in the fire was used on Daniel, as well.

The administrators set to serve under the current reign of King Darius were bent on removing Daniel from his seat. Daniel had found favor with King Nebuchadnezzar and King Belshazzar prior to King Darius' reign through his interpretation of dreams and godly wisdom.

So, they convinced the king to "issue an edict and enforce the decree that anyone who prays to any god or man during the next thirty days, except to you, O king, shall be thrown into the lions den" *(Daniel 6:7)*. The king, not realizing that the "royal administrators, prefects, satraps, advisers and governors have all agreed …"(6:7) did not include Daniel, agreed.

The rest is history. We read in Daniel 6 the infamous story of Daniel's bravery in the face of his choice to worship the Lord over the law (6: 10). The king, distraught over the decree he was tricked into issuing *(Daniel 6:14),* nevertheless sealed Daniel into the lion's den (v. 17). Unable to eat or sleep (v. 18), the king rushed to the den at dawn. "Daniel, servant of the living God, has your God, whom you serve continually, been able to rescue you from the lions?" (vv. 19-20)

"My God sent his angel, and he shut the mouths of the lions," came Daniel's reply from the den.
The decree was reversed, requiring all in the land to worship God, and those who had conspired against Daniel were tossed into the lion's den.

The Prayer that Shut Mouths

When we are pressed up against troubling times, let us look to Daniel's example of how to gather strength in distress. Turning to God for justice and answers was not new territory for him. It was habit. He prayed habitually. He looked to the Lord routinely.

If we establish a daily habit of turning to God in our lives, it's more likely to be our immediate reaction in times of trouble. There is no way around spending time with God: we must have a relationship with Him in order to experience His peace. We must spend time in the Word. We must spend time in prayer. Pausing to look at our current situation in the light of His perspective is the essential path to taking hold of His peace.

Christ died to give us full access to our great God. We can look to His Word, look up to Him in prayer, and embrace the power of the Holy Spirit at work within us. The societal misconception is that we possess the strength to pull ourselves out of trouble. But if we rely on our own strength, we'll surely fail. It's His strength that makes our salvation possible. Walking with Christ isn't about striving for perfection, but straining towards submission. [6]

The New Glasses

When I finally broke down and got new glasses, I went all out. I let my doctor fit lenses that would stop headaches and cut the glare of the sun.

"He came into the very world he created, but the world didn't recognize him. He came to his own people, and even they rejected him. But to all who believed him and accepted him, he gave the right to become children of God. They are reborn—not with a physical birth resulting from human passion or plan, but a birth that comes from God." John 1:10-13

Each morning, I faithfully clean and prepare my glasses for the day with special cloth and spray. Its worth it to me. I appreciate the view. Guess what? They're shatterproof, too. My new vision is as protected as it could possibly be.

When Zechariah lost his ability to see God clearly, he lost his speech along with it. He doubted the vision he saw. He questioned the message. At his son's birth, his speech was restored. Jesus restored our hope with His. Might something left previously out of focus, now be revealed as a blind spot from seeing gods hand in our situation?

The b-side of birth lies beyond God's creation of our physicality. He built the possibility of hope into our DNA. A gift of grace allowed by the sacrifice of that baby boy born in the town of David. The

---

[6] "A Prayer for God's Help in Times of Trouble," Meg Bucher, **crosswalk.com**

opportunity to break free and follow Him home. The power of purpose as our feet tread the dirt of this Earth. When Christ is our personal Savior, the silence is lifted from our souls and our vision realigned …like getting new glasses. In a fresh hug of friendship defined, we are born …again.

Believe. See…

We have this view of friendship that has to fit the mold we want to squeeze it into. Our friends have to be loyal to us, share similar interests, and align with every argument and beef we have with someone. How sad that really is.

For God's definition of friendship is so starkly different. God-placed friendships move the kingdom agenda forward, not our own personal agenda.

The three friends being appointed by Daniel had little to do with their personal relationship to each other, and everything to do with who met them in that fire. Do we believe that God will meet us in the fire? And if we do, are we aware that He sometimes surrounds us with friends as we walk through it? Sometimes, we bond for life over shared encounters with Him.

Friendship is God-placed for His glory, out of His love for us. He is jealous for us, and pursues us. Our earthly friendships are not what we make of them. When we let them be what God intends, they are the true extension of His love to us.

Our Father knows it's not good for us to be alone. Though He is our best friend, our earthly friendships are the gift of His pursuit of our hearts. If we choose to see them for what they are. Facing out ward and upward.

Let's Pray …

Father,

*Praise You for the friends that You place along the way in our lives. Your omnipotence is evident in the consistent and constant way You provide comfort and encouragement alongside discipline, perfecting us in faith until the day we hug you in heaven. There are some days that we don't feel like facing, want to face, or know how we will make it to the end of. In those moments, we can cry out to you ...in the ugliest and most desperate ways. We can hit our knees, collapse in agony, and know without a shadow of a doubt that Jesus has a hand our shoulder as we sob. For **"He reveals deep and hidden things; he knows what lies in the darkness, and light dwells with him." -Daniel 2:22***

You know what we need and who is primed to extend Your love for us at any given moment. You go before us and behind us, and prepare the way for us. How great is Your love?! It's huge! It's incomprehensible to us. It's overwhelming and exhilarating all at the same time. You are so good, Father. Thank You for caring for us through others. Help us to see those that You place to comfort and encourage, and comfort us with our dysfunction. Give us more of the Holy Spirit so that we can recognize Your guiding hand. As we seek more of You. More of Jesus. More of the Holy Spirit, help us to understand these words:

"He came into the very world he created, but the world didn't recognize him. He came to his own people, and even they rejected him. But to all who believed him and accepted him, he gave the right to become children of God. They are reborn—not with a physical birth resulting from human passion or plan, but a birth that comes from God." John 1:10-13

From God. From You. Help us to turn and run from our sin and obediently to You. Bless us to be a good and faithful servant, spreading Your love and encouragement, confronting dysfunction, and providing comfort for those in need of companionship. Guide us, and soften our hearts and tune our ears to listen, move, and go.

In Jesus' Name,
Amen.

Section Three

Forming and Fostering Healthy Friendships

Chapter 7

Intro to A.R.M.
(Attain, Retain, Maintain)

Now that we've learned how to define friendship by God's standards, and learned that part of His pursuit of us comes through the people He places in our lives, let's talk about how we form and foster healthy friendships.

Though God did not create us to be alone, we certainly would rather operate that way most of the time. We are wired to want our way, and gravitate towards people who have views and opinions that align with our own. Our culture pushes us to be independent, and to live our individual truth. Since no two people are alike, and we all fall short, we've set ourselves up for an immediate let down when it comes to our relationships.

The Independant

"So he was despised and forsaken by men, this man of suffering, grief's patient friend." Isaiah 53:3 (VOICE)

Independence can become an obsession if we believe we're entitled to it. As the world gets bigger and bigger, and our reach to communicate across it get's smaller and smaller, the freedom to reach out is easier than ever to grasp.

independent- not subject to control by others. Merriam-Webster

The human reflex for control confuses what it means to be free. God, who created everything and everyone, is in control, but He's not a controlling God. The Bible tells the story of His grace, but it's our choice to accept it.

"There was nothing beautiful or majestic about his appearance, nothing to attract us to him.

He was despised and rejected—a man of sorrows, acquainted with deepest grief.
We turned our backs on him and looked the other way.

He was despised, and we did not care."

Isaiah 53:2b-3

The prophet Isaiah is describing Jesus. There are over thirty-five New Testament references reflected back to Isaiah, Chapter 53. Jesus truly is the Word. The more I study it, the more I see Him in every verse. And if I don't see Him, I start to search ...knowing He's there.

The Way, The Truth, and the Life. Our Independence. Our Freedom.

Jesus (thinking of John the Baptist): Elijah does come first to restore all things. They have it right. But there is something else written in the Scriptures about the Son of Man: He will have to suffer and be rejected. Mark 9:12

God is not controlling, but He is in control. Jesus bought our freedom on the cross. Grace aims to free everyone ...leaving no one behind. In order for our relationships to reflect our freedom, we have to free our friends.

I would have never chosen to read through the book of 1 Kings …let alone 2 Kings, too, if my daily devotional program wouldn't have taken me down that road. But as God always does, He met me there with an important message.

I can be like those dysfunctional kings.
I began to highlight the beginning of each new reign, all the way up to the last King, King Zedekiah.

"Zedekiah was twenty-one years old when he became king, and he reigned in Jerusalem eleven years. His mother's name was Hamutal daughter of Jeremiah; she was from Libnah." 2 Kings 24: 18 (NIV)

Reign after reign began with the same writing on the wall …

" He did evil in the eyes of the Lord, just as Jehoikim ha done."

"It was because of the Lord's anger that all this happened to Jerusalem and Judah, and in the end he thrust them from his presence."
2 Kings 24:19- 20 (NIV)

Over and over again, even after some amazing stories of redemption and restoration, the next king would come along and wreck all progress, reverting back to the bad habits of previous generations.

How was God telling me that I was like those dysfunctional kings? Because no matter how many times my running to other people before running to God let me to a dead end, I continued to run into those walls. Every time I tried to hold tight to God's standards for my life, the next set of trying circumstances and pressures would send me running again. And it was ruining my friendships.

My friends were never meant to be my savior. Jesus is my Savior. I know that. But my heart's initial reaction wasn't reflecting it. I look back at every friendship I ruined by my dysfunction. Each time, I let my self-centered need in that friendship come before God's ordained purpose for it.

Why do we assume friendship is always comfortable? That we'll always agree? That we'll happily skip down the road arm in arm as BFF's forever and ever and nothing will ever come between us?

….but we do. And we get seriously aggravated when that pretty little pedestal gets knocked down to the ground. When we feel like we need space, instead of overextending ourselves for a friend who desperately needs us. When we look at our phone and decide not to answer that text at all, knowing full well feelings are hurting on the other end because of it. Committing to too many plans and ghosting the runner-up because we can't say no or admit that we over-scheduled. Rather, we selfishly pick the option that sounds more fun.

Oh, I will creep into all of the uncomfortable crevices of friendship with you, because I have been through the friendship ringer …on both sides and in the middle. One doesn't live a life mantra to be friends with everyone without getting scorched, and starting some fires along the way. I wrestled until I realized where I needed to run.

After the last big friendship blow-out in my life, I decided I needed to set some serious God-based standards to protect myself and my family, and to protect others from being hurt by my misaimed friendship arrows. All of those dysfunctional kings taught me that I didn't want to be known by that kind of legacy. The kind of friend who only put others first when it was convenient, or ran from conflict.

And then one day He pressed upon my heart …

"Run to me …hard and fast. Run to ME."

Jesus loves us for who we are, right where we are at. God showed me how to keep myself in check and outward facing in friendship, by running to Him.

A.R.M.

Attain. Retain. Maintain.

"Listen to advice and accept discipline, and at the end you will be counted among the wise." Proverbs 19:20 (NIV)

We need wisdom to form healthy friendships. And it's not our wisdom we need to tap into, but God's. Scripture is alive and active. It's God's way of communicating with us, guiding us, teaching us, and so much more. The Bible is everything. And yes, it can help us make friends, find friends, be good friends and get to know our best Friend. If we're not reading it, we'll never find the right answers.

The Voice in My Car

"Re-routing, ...WHAT!?!?"

My daughter rolled laughing as she caught my google aimed rant on a mom/daughter road trip. Have you ever followed google maps down a road that you feel is against your better judgement? Ever wish you could pull off to the side of the road, minimize the map and make sure that google has, in fact, picked the best route? Me, too. But I'm afraid of "rerouting ...."

I can tell she's mad at me when I don't follow her directions, and inside all of us is the desire to go with the flow. It's hard to make a bold move against the google girl because our sense of direction is kicking in. But every time I fail to follow my gut instinct, I end up lost. Most recently, turned around in the countryside of North Carolina, in the pouring rain. One country back road after the next, all because I didn't make that U Turn google begged me to make. Had I done so, I would have experienced the much more direct route I drove on the way back that night. All that twisting and turning just because I was afraid to make a U-turn.

How do we know when to reroute, and when to trust and stay on the suggested course? On the road of friendship, the only way to know what lane to stay in is by elevating the volume of His voice above all others. Even google. Pray into, about, over, and through friendship.

God showed me that in order to attain, retain, and maintain friendships, prayer time and chair time in God's Word has to be a priority. The priority. We're all busy. It sounds impossible to get up even thirty seconds earlier than we already do in the morning ...but going out into the world blind is downright dangerous.

Pop a preacher in your ear buds while you brush your teeth. In the time it takes to sit down and pee in the morning, one day's worth of a Jesus Calling devotional can be digested (Maybe TMI, but speaking from experience, here!.) There's simply no way around it. No substitution for it. We have to be in the word. It's really not too much to ask. Jesus died horrifically so that we can do just that. Talk to God. Pray. Read the Bible. He didn't make that possible so that we would feel guilty and pressed for time to squeeze Him into our lives. Holy cow, do we get it twisted.

The stark difference in who I am now compared to who I was a decade ago is due to the time I choose to give to Him every morning. I get made fun of, as if it's unrealistic and impossible. But let me tell you, the God who made time will stretch yours to fit time with Him in.

To attain friends, I had to learn what friendship meant from God's point of view. I began to pray for my friends and my friendships. I prayed for godly friends and God-centered friendships. I prayed for mentors and for others to encourage. Prayer is the first step to attain healthy friendships. We don't just want to accumulate people like they are collectors items. We don't want our friendships to be forced. We want genuine, loyal, and purposed friendships. And to attract that kind of friendship, we have to be that kind of friend.

Selfless.

When we run to God first, He will flip our perspective to a servant standpoint rather than a self-consumed priorities. He opens our eyes to the purpose of friendship. We can retain those friends because, with a selfless attitude, we're not clutching to them for our every need. And we can maintain those friendships, because we can flow in and out of them without worry about it falling a part. The freedom of God-placed friends takes that pressure off of us. It's a whole lot less about what kind of friend we are and what kind of friend they are to us, and more about how God has brought us together. How can I help this friend and then …what …another friend sees my need and helps me.

Selfless. That's the key. Choosing not to be offended by every missed call, and instead trusting God's placement of people in our lives.

Standards. If we are being taken advantage of, do we trust that God will alert us, and can we disengage from that friendship if we have to? Can we let go without making it personal? Even if it is?

The Selfless Servant

Elisha had the privilege of training and serving alongside the great prophet Elijah. When it was time for Elijah to move on to the next town, he instructed his servant to stay behind.

"As surely as the Lord lives and as you live, I will not leave you,"Elisha replied. (2 Kings 2:2)

He knew what was about to happen, and though Elijah asked him twice more to stay behind, he kept going. (**2 Kings 2:3**) Had Elisha stayed behind, he never would have witnessed the miracles that followed. Elijah rolled up his cloak, hit the Jordan river, and it parted for the two to walk across. (**2 Kings 2:7-8**) As they chatted as two old friends, chariots of fire separated them, and Elijah was taken up in a whirlwind to be with God. (**2 Kings 2:9-12**)

Friendship is filled with hard moments that make us question whether or not the other person is worth the outpouring of our loyalty. If we follow God's leading in the midst of those hesitations, I believe we will experience the miracle of selfless love on this earth and what He can do through it. [7]Adversely, He may caution us to put the brakes on …to avoid incoming hurt.

If we set our focus only on what we can extract from friendship, we will miss the freedom and peace of abiding solely in Him.

The Friendship Path

"Those who live right are good guides to those who follow, but wrongdoers will steer their friends down the wrong path."
Proverbs 12:26

If we look back on each friendship that's touched our lives, we can trace a path.

Friendships that are built on solid foundations seem forever unbreakable. But cracks in the fault of a trusting relationship can prove irreconcilable. We can step over them and continue on, but there's no going back to retrace faltered steps. The mistakes we

---

[7] "10 Friendships from the Bible to Learn from," https://www.crosswalk.com/slideshows/10-friendships-of-the-bible-to-learn-from.html

make with our friends' hearts cannot be unwound or undone. The forward falling nature of life will continue to tumble on.

Psalm 12:26 reminds us to be smart about the friendships we form and alert to the methods in which we maintain those friendships. It's necessary to form some healthy boundaries against behaviors that may jeopardize the people we are aiming to become. But be wise not to loft a 'better than' attitude or build a judgmental platform of friendship qualifications. We're to remain in the world, but not of it.

God wants us to use caution in the time we spend marinating our hearts in the world, before we begin to take on a completely different flavor. That takes trusting in God's timing in our lives, and in the lives of others. He's working in all of us, simultaneously, but we're not all meant to collide at the same time. When we walk with Christ, we are on path to holiness that leads to heaven. Along that path, God will litter our lives with others that are on that same sojourn. We can know when to linger and when to leave by listening to what we've already learned about God and people.

1   *Friends will come in God's time.* Staying focused on Him will allow us to see the people He has brought into our lives to help …and others that are there to help us.

2   *Friendships need to breathe.* Conversation with friends shouldn't take precedent over the time we spend with God. Filling up with His Word first will allow us to have healthy friendships.

3   *Friends encourage and sharpen.* Godly friends will encourage us in our relationship with God, and call us into accountability through the love of God's Word. Christ is not at the center of a friendship that leads us away from Him.

When considering who to spend our minutes with, it's important to remind ourselves what we're here for.

Let's Pray …

Father,
Praise You for Your timing. Creator of time, You can stretch our
minutes, speed up our suffering, and spin the earth in it's seasons.
Perfectly just and right, Your timing is good because You are good.
You are love. Jesus came in perfect timing, to save us all …but also
to suffer. Help us to reflect on the words of Isaiah as we pray, today:

"So he was despised and forsaken by men, this man of suffering,
grief's patient friend." Isaiah 53:3 (VOICE
"There was nothing beautiful or majestic about his appearance,
nothing to attract us to him.
He was despised and rejected—a man of sorrows, acquainted with
deepest grief.
We turned our backs on him and looked the other way.

Father, sometimes we fail to understand the gravity of Jesus'
suffering. Not only was it physically brutal and unthinkably painful,
but **"He was despised, and we did not care." Isaiah 53:2b-3** *He*
suffered emotionally. When we fail to remember that He knows how
we feel, remind us, Father, that, **"He will have to suffer and be**
rejected." Mark 9:12

Jesus loves us with a compassion that we cannot fathom. We deserve
death for our sin, and He chose to die to wipe away our rightful
punishment. The One who didn't have to suffer choose to. And not
just physically, but the nasty, emotionally manipulating and bullying
way we mock and make fun. Torn down by those He would hang for.
Even now, we run from Him, Father, though He waits for us to
accept His gift of salvation and grace. Thank You, Father, for
pursing us when we run away from You.

Fix the broken parts of our hearts that damage those You have
placed in our care to love. Forgive us, Father, for gossip and

jealousy, bitterness and manipulation. Help us to honor and glorify You through the way we treat people. Help us to love people like You do. Friendship is an opportunity to do just that. Yet, so many times, we are faced inward with selfish motivations that prevent us from serving those people the way we should. Help us to remember these words, and apply them actively to our lives and friendships:

"Listen to advice and accept discipline, and at the end you will be counted among the wise." *Proverbs 19:20 (NIV)*

"Those who live right are good guides to those who follow, but wrongdoers will steer their friends down the wrong path." *Proverbs 12:26*

Father, we pray today to lead lives that reflect Your love and grace. May the joy that we have in You be evident to all ...not just in what we say, but in how we live.

In Jesus' Name,
Amen.

Chapter 8

Attain: Making Friends
(Don't Pee on People.)

Don't pee on me.

Have you ever felt like your being marked as part of someone's property? Had to strive for permission to step into another's self-proclaimed territory?

"You are my friends." John 15:14 (NIV)

What are we doing with our friendships? What standards are we walking out into the world with when we consider who we call our friends? And are we taking into consideration what Jesus meant when He said, *"I call you friends?"*

Jesus said, *"You didn't choose me, I chose you."*

He didn't choose us because He needed us. When we look at the way Jesus formed His earthly friendships, we understand His character and purpose for calling us friends, and what our responsibility on earth is when we consider our friendships. [8]

---

[8] "Who Were Jesus' Friends?" https://www.crosswalk.com/faith/bible-study/who-were-jesus-friends.html

The Friend Goal

Why attain friends? What is the goal of accumulating friends on this earth? We're not assured to experience less loneliness when surrounded by friends. In fact, pockets of transition between friends have been some of the loneliest times in my life. I LOVE people. Part of the 20% of the world's population that carries the Highly Sensitive Person gene, I'm also the 30% of that 20% that are extroverted. I cherish my friendships and ...if I'm not careful ...put them first.

For me, everything about friendship is intensified. Maybe that's why I've been tasked to write a book about friendship. Because I notice more than the other 80% of the population. It can be overwhelming if I don't take captive every distorted and runaway thought that filters through my mind when I'm with a group of friends or out on social media. But the cool thing about it is the benefit I can pass on to the other 80% that don't see what I see. Imagine, even more so, the wisdom we gain when we surrender to God, who knows all, sees all, and sits above all.

It's important to consider what friendship meant in Biblical times. The NIV Cultural Backgrounds Study Bible states that *"the language of friendship was applied to patron-client relationships, in which patrons supplied some needs of clients."* NKJV Chronological Study Bible Notes says, *"In the Roman world, a 'friend' was often a political ally who owed one a favor, or a more powerful patron on whom one could depend."*[9]

We do aim to accumulate rather than attain, don't we? There is safety in numbers, acceptance, in our crew. We tend to linger in a pocket of comfortable, like-minded believers. But we can't. We have to pop out of our comfort zone in order to minister to those God has

---

9

placed on our radar. Approaching friendship with a servant, outward facing attitude, allows us to enlarge our circle by shrinking our focus. He broadens our horizon by removing us from our comfort zone.

Jesus had a close circle of twelve on this earth, but He calls *us friends*, too. The NKJV Chronological Bible Notes for this verse explain, *"While He was not implying that His friends were His equals, He was offering to share with them what belonged to Him."* And the second half of **John 15:14, *"You are my friends, if you do what I command,"*** gives us a good glimpse into the Christly perspective of friendship. [10]

People tend to "pack" up. Friends are important, but our friends are people, too. When we focus too much on claiming our place in another life, or assigning them a role in ours, we strangle our own growth. Whoever devotes themselves to themselves will have nothing but themselves to show for themselves.

We don't often think of the friends of Jesus as political allies or business acquaintances. Jesus took a concept familiar to those that surrounded Him at the time, and redefined what it meant to be a friend. *"Jesus is our model for love… If believers obey His command to love, they enjoy the intimacy of His friendship. Friendship …is not a once-for-all gift, but develops as the result of obeying Jesus' command to love."* NKJV Study Bible [11]

King David, the original "I want to be friends with everyone," had a heart after God's very own. He meant well. I can relate to this. I am the master at finding something positive about everyone, to the fault that my acceptance can be misconstrued as alignment to their beliefs.

---

[10] "Who Were Jesus Friends?"https://www.crosswalk.com/faith/bible-study/who-were-jesus-friends.html

[11] "Who Were Jesus' Friends?" https://www.crosswalk.com/faith/bible-study/who-were-jesus-friends.html

Evangelism is not a strong point of mine. I have an extremely hard time stopping in my tracks and saying, *"No, you're wrong. There's one God. My God. The God. The Father, Son, and the Holy Spirit. And Jesus? Not just a guy. I'm sorry, you're wrong. He's my Savior. He's your Savior. He's the way, the truth, and the life. No one comes to the Father accept through Him."*

My soul is screaming it at a distorted volume, but my dysfunctional desire to please people gets in the way. We can still be friends with everyone without losing our conviction in Christ. We can love everyone without agreeing with everyone. God's standards can reign true in my life if I step aside and let Him work.

Attain: to reach, achieve, or accomplish; gain; obtain. (*dictionary.com*)

In our quest to find the right way to form new friendships, God asks three questions:

1. What's our angle?

There are many Proverbs that guide us to align our friendships with God's truth. If it's anything self-seeking or self-gratifying, let it lie. There is a definite reason that God brings people into our lives, but if there's just a juicy piece of gossip that we really want to extract over a cup of coffee, then cancel that date.

"Walk with the wise and become wise, for a companion of fools suffers harm." Proverbs 13:20 (NIV)

When we want the recognition of association or the ability to name-drop, walk away. Pray into friendship. Ask God to illuminate the reason this person has stepped onto our horizon.

"The mocker seeks wisdom and finds none, but knowledge comes easily to the discerning. Stay away from a fool, for you will not find knowledge on their lips." Proverbs 14:6-7 (NIV)

Eliminate self-seeking efforts to connect, network, associate, and gain …anything …other than honest conversation and the allowance of God to unravel His purpose for that friendship.

"Do not make friends with a hot-tempered person, do not associate with one easily angered, or you may learn their ways and get yourself ensnared." Proverbs 22: 24-25 (NIV)

God, who tells us not to judge for He is the only just judge, threw standards of friendship into Scripture for our own good. Only He knows what is going on in everyone's lives and hearts. He knows who we need and who needs us. Not every encounter is a meant to be deep friendship. We aren't friendship failures for falling in and out of a few friendships. Our place in another's life is God's ordination, not our own.

We're not to judge, but we are to have standards. Our lives cannot be subject to sway to every whim that crosses our path. Sometimes, we are meant to be the ones that encourage others to level up. Other times, we need a leveling.

It's OK to say, *"I love you, but I can't go there with you."* Not all situations in life revolve primarily around us. Often, we're caught up in our own pain …our own end of the struggle ..too much to see the good God is pulling out of it. And our lives bear witness to the inward focus we are bent on.

"Be joyful always." 1 Thessalonians 5:16

We have no authority to judge, but every reason to be joyful. The strength that it takes to extract joy in hard circumstances comes from Him. Sometimes from that "level up" challenge from a friend. Or, that "do you realize that you rock at this," from a mentor. Good and God ordained friendships may not always be comfortable, but they don't conflict with what God says about us ...or them.

The Twelve

"Greater love has no one than this: to lay down one's life for one's friends." John 15:13 (NIV)

Loyalty and the sharing of secrets were important to ancient friendships, and the Greeks held the expression to die for a friend the highest expression of loyalty. *(NKFV Notes)* Jesus took care in choosing those closest to Him. *"Disciples of teachers were like apprentices; the best could ideally carry on the teacher's work." (NIV SB)*

"Here are the names of the twelve apostles: first, Simon (also called Peter), then Andrew (Peter's brother), James (son of Zebedee), John (James's brother), Philip, Bartholomew, Thomas, Matthew (the tax collector), James (son of Alphaeus), Thaddaeus," Matthew 10:2-3

The apostles held no qualifications to be apprentice to the Savior of the world. They were average men, at best. But Jesus saw something in them, as He does in us, unknown even to them. They left everything to follow Him, and with that simple step of obedience He molded them into fishers of men. [12]

2. What's their angle?

Discernment is the ability to detect genuine kindness. *2 Peter 1: 5-7* states, *"For this very reason, make every effort to add to your faith goodness; and to goodness, knowledge; and to knowledge, self-*

---

[12] "Who Were Jesus' Friends?" https://www.crosswalk.com/faith/bible-study/who-were-jesus-friends.html

control; and to self-control, perseverance; and to perseverance, godliness; and to godliness, brotherly kindness; and to brotherly kindness, love."

Friends bring out and admonish those qualities in us. Sometimes, challenging or confronting us to level-up where we are struggling or scared to move forward, or falling short.

James 1:2-4 states, "Consider it pure joy, my brothers, whenever you face trials of many kinds, because you know the testing of your faith develops perseverance. Perseverance must finish its work so that you may be mature and complete, not lacking anything."

Friends can also deliver trials, or face them with us. It's not always easy. Easy shouldn't be the number one requirement of friendship. But if it's not growing us, refining us, or pressing us through, we should use caution to make sure it's not pushing us away from Christ.

Our faith can help us to discern genuine kindness from fake or false intentions. When we seek God first, I believe He warns us. But I, for one, don't always listen. I'm too busy trying to focus on the best, lest I become labeled "unaccepting" of everyone's truth. But when that warning goes off, it's God trying to protect us.

"The righteous choose their friends carefully, but the way of the wicked leads them astray." Proverbs 12:26 (NIV)

Be wary and very prayerful and cautious when the question of someone's genuine kindness lingers thick in the air. There may be a rich and rewarding friendship down the road, or it could just be a moment of ministry. The key is to give every relationship to God, and line it up against His standards. We can do this by praying to have ears to hear and eyes to see true intentions.

"You, dear children, are from God and have overcome them, because the one who is in you is greater than the one who is in the world.
They are from the world and therefore speak from the viewpoint of the world, and the world listens to them.

We are from God, and whoever knows God listens to us; but whoever is not from God does not listen to us. This is how we recognize the Spirit of truth and the spirit of falsehood."
1 John 4:4-6 (NIV)

The Big Three

Of the twelve disciples, Scripture reveals a lot about Jesus' friendships with Peter, James and John. James and John were brothers, and the three of them had been called to follow Christ while out fishing on John's father's boat. *(Luke 5:1-11)*

These three were present for miracles that the others were not. Jesus specifically brings only those three along with him to Jarius' house, where He raised his daughter from the dead. *"He allowed no one to go with Him but Peter and James and John." Mark 5:37 (NIV)* They were also taken up the mountain for the miraculous transfiguration of Jesus. *"Jesus took with Him Peter and James and his brother John." Matthew 17:1*

They all turned out to be big time leaders of the early church. Though we are all followers of Jesus, not all are called to lead the founding of churches and write Gospel accounts. Perhaps Jesus took the extra care to personalize their apprenticeship, knowing what lied ahead of them.[13]

3. Why Me?

---

[13] "Who Were Jesus Friends?" https://www.crosswalk.com/faith/bible-study/who-were-jesus-friends.html

"When tempted, no one should say 'God is tempting me.' for God cannot be tempted by evil, nor does he tempt anyone; but each one is tempted when by his own even desire, he is dragged away and enticed." James 1:13-14 (NIV)

The word "trials" is the same Greek word for "tempted." In English, trials and temptations seem similar but not the same. But to God, they are. He sees all sins through the same just lens. The exterior trials from peer and societal pressure, and the inner bent towards sin that we all struggle with. Both are equally dangerous to our lives, and they will take us out if we lack godly perseverance.

2 Peter 1:5-7 stresses the importance of perseverance. *"For this very reason, make every effort to add to your faith goodness; and to goodness, knowledge, and to knowledge, self-control; and to self-control, perseverance, and to perseverance, godliness; and to godliness, mutual affection; and to mutual affection, love."*

Scripture is showing us that to even begin to persevere through the kinds of trials and temptations that will ultimately mature our faith completely, we have to have faith. *(cue George Micheal ...the nineties are back.)* It starts with faith, and then we add to faith goodness ...self control ...and then perseverance. Only then, can we move forward to what perseverance produces, godliness ...kindness ...and love.

Why us? How do we recognize the common ground God put us on to foster friendship?

The One Jesus Loved

The Apostle John referred to himself as *"the one Jesus loved,"(John 14:13)* as He reclined on Him at the Last Supper. But John's loyalty as a friend to Jesus surpassed his speech. He was there for Him in the Garden, and the only one of the twelve at the foot of the cross.

"When Jesus saw his mother there, and the disciple whom he loved standing nearby, he said to his mother, 'Dear woman, here is your son, and to the disciple, 'Here is your mother.' From that time on this disciple took her into his home." John 19:26-27 (NIV)

He was called just like the other twelve, and witnessed miracles alongside the big three. John, however, was the only apostle that wasn't martyred. He was given the vision that we study in the book of Revelation. John wrote something particularly touching of Jesus as He began to retell of the foot washing at the Last Supper.

"Having loved his own who were in the world, he now showed them the full extent of his love." John 13:1b

Perhaps John was the most eloquent with words, among his other gifts. Though we get a very matter of fact view of the gospel account from Mark, John wrote a palpable picture of what it felt to like to be close to Jesus. An important quality to embrace and understand as we seek our own friendship with Him.[14]

The Real-time Race Start

I believe that these verses lead us to an important key in unlocking a healthy attainment of friendships. Faith comes from being with God, in His Word. It's a sitting with Him and waiting to be developed process. But the outcome that beads up from that investment of time is goodness. And that goodness rolls off into self-control. Any athlete knows that self-control fuels perseverance.

---

[14] "Who Were Jesus' Friends?" https://www.crosswalk.com/faith/bible-study/who-were-jesus-friends.html

I was a distance runner in college, and none of us stepped to the line in May for the first time. We'd been stepping to the line mentally since December. We'd been preparing, training, visualizing, strengthening …and moving towards our race goals long before the gun went off. That same self-control fuels the movement and growth God is calling us to by allowing us to persevere through the trials and temptations that He has prepared us to face.

Moments of preparation lead to life's crossroads, where we get to extend the hope stored in us to another child of God coming home for the first time. Maybe it's just a timely hug, text, note, or call.

Coming through endurance-producing seasons with Christ produces godliness. We aspire to be more like Him because we've experienced His power moving through us. And it causes our hearts to begin to mirror His kindness and love, little by little.

Faith. Goodness. Self-control. Perseverance. Godliness. Kindness. Love. It takes a whole lot of effort to produce a single note of kindness. It's not of this world. Sometimes, it takes a trial to change our hearts.

Before I claimed the label "divorce" it was hard for me not to judge. Not because I thought I was better than, I just didn't understand. My own trial produced compassion for those going through it alongside and after me. He reached down and scooped me out of my mess, and put the pieces back together. I get it, now. And it produced kindness and love that is not from me, but from Christ.

Perhaps when we lack or struggle in these areas we are failing to look back and fully embrace God's forgiveness. 2 Peter 1:9 says, *"But if anyone does not have them, he is nearsighted and blind, and he's forgotten that tone has been cleansed from his past sins."*

Yes, we forget. When we look to attain friends for convenience or confidence, we are getting it wrong. Moreover, we may miss the honor to minister to the people God has placed in our paths.

The goal of friendship by God's standards is to reach, achieve, or accomplish …gain …obtain …His goals. His purposes. It has everything to do with His love for His people. When we truly care for those He has placed in our paths, He promises to do more than we can ask for or imagine. Sometimes, He'll minister to us … confront us …and other times, we will have the opportunity to come alongside another one of His beloved and serve them as a friend. Comfort them and tell them that God is bigger and Jesus never left them. Invite them over for dinner. Take them to church. Go walk the pier. Have coffee.

"If anyone has material possessions and sees a brother or sister in need but has no pity on them, how can the love of God be in that person?" 1 John 3:17 (NIV)

The Friends that Felt Like Family

Jesus' friendship with these three siblings began with hospitality. *"As Jesus and his disciples were on their way, he came to a village where a woman named Martha opened her home to him." Luke 10:38 (NIV)* Jesus taught a distracted Martha to sit still in His presence. All of our friendships can be improved upon by sitting still with Jesus.

Later on in the Gospel accounts, the two sisters run to Jesus when their brother Lazarus is sick. *"Lord, the one you love is sick." John 11:3 (NIV)* Jesus goes before us, and knows more about what we need than we do. He wept for what His friends had to go through to get to the miracle. (John 11:35) There will always be an inevitable thread of suffering in our sin-laden world, but the hope of Jesus cannot be trumped by any temporary pain on earth. Overwhelming as seemingly unfair as life can and will be at times, we can trust our friend, Jesus, as Mary and Martha and Lazarus learned to do.[15]

Be available to the people God is placing in your path. Many of our friends will be God-placed when we're not looking. And every friendship we force will most likely fall a part. *"God's kind of love, which he pours out in the believer's heart and which in turn enables the Christian to love fellow believers. Or it may speak of the believers love for God."* NIV Study Bible Notes on 1John 3:17

Our attainment of friends reflects our acknowledgement of His love, alive and active in our lives. It's not choosy, it's inclusive. It's not discriminatory, it's welcoming. His love is where we set our aim in attaining friends.

Let's Pray ...

Father,

Praise You for Jesus' friendship. It's an unbelievable extension of Your love. We don't deserve it. We can't earn it. We don't even know what to do with it, we are so floored by it, sometimes. But you warn us to be careful when opening the doors wide open to our hearts, **"The righteous choose their friends carefully, but the way of the wicked leads them astray." Proverbs 12:26 (NIV)** *It is by that knowledge that we pray for, today, Father. Bless our hearts to receive it.*

Jesus calls us friends. **"You are my friends." John 15:14 (NIV)** *Jesus loved His friends on earth. He gave us so many examples of friendship, and His expectations and guidelines for it.* **"Having loved his own who were in the world, he now showed them the full extent of his love." John 13:1b**

---

[15] "Who Were Jesus' Friends?" https://www.crosswalk.com/faith/bible-study/who-were-jesus-friends.html

Father, You have left us a multitude of wisdom concerning what to beware of when befriending others. There is a way to extend Your love for them without comprising the status of our souls, but it's hard. And, it's impossible to live out honestly without Your constant and consistent guidance.

The only way to tune in is through Your Word. Help us to focus and listen to what You say in Proverbs 14:6-7: **"The mocker seeks wisdom and finds none, but knowledge comes easily to the discerning. Stay away from a fool, for you will not find knowledge on their lips."(NIV)** and, **Proverbs 22:24-35:"Do not make friends with a hot-tempered person, do not associate with one easily angered, or you may learn their ways and get yourself ensnared." (NIV)**

We can be so easily ensnared by the enemy's lies, because he butts so closely to the Truth. Help us to stay in the Word daily, so we can thwart the enemies attacks. They are sneaky and deceitful, and sometimes we can throw ourselves right into his devious plans by dulling our senses to God's wisdom. As we pray these verses today, protect our hearts and guard our minds, filling them both with the truth of Your wisdom, so that our friendships will be genuine.

2 Peter 1: 5-7 states, "For this very reason, make every effort to add to your faith goodness; and to goodness, knowledge; and to knowledge, self-control; and to self-control, perseverance; and to perseverance, godliness; and to godliness, brotherly kindness; and to brotherly kindness, love."

Guide us to the Truth, and open our ears to hear James 1:2-4, **"Consider it pure joy, my brothers, whenever you face trials of many kinds, because you know the the testing of your faith develops perseverance. Perseverance must finish its work so that you may be mature and complete, not lacking anything."**

In Jesus' Name,
Amen.

Chapter 9

Retain: Keeping Friends
(Everyone has a Ruth ...and We've all had Naomi days.)

After studying David and Jonathan's friendship, we are going to dive into Ruth's loyal friendship to Naomi. Ruth was David's great-great grandma. Our God is not one of coincidence, and I love how these two stories of friendship connect two distinctly different generations.

Ruth refuses to leave Naomi. Even after her husband has died and she has no ties to her mother-in-law, she does not leave her. Naomi pleads with her, and in dramatic fashion proclaims,

"Return home, my daughters. Why would you come with me? Am I going to have any more sons, who could become your husbands? Return home, my daughters; I am too old to have another husband.
Even if I thought there was still hope for me-even if I had a husband tonight and then gave birth to sons- would you wait until they grew up? Would you remain unmarried for them? No, my daughters. It is more bitter for me than for you, because the Lord's hand has gone out against me!"
Ruth 1:11-13

I've had Naomi days. Days when I wept on the floor and couldn't dream of how God would stand me back up again. After my divorce,

I became a ghost. Social media wasn't a huge thing yet, and I was able to change a phone number and an email and virtually disappear. I didn't want to talk about it. I didn't want to feel guilty about it. And I didn't want to be judged.

The flip-side to going through what others can only speculate is the hurtful realization of what they're saying about us. How quickly we jump from one side of the conversation to the other sometimes, and how quickly everyone forgets who we really are. How tragically, we can forget who Christ says we are.

Ruth did not. She stayed. In fact, she *"clung."* She remembered who Naomi was. And she knew her place as her friend.

"Don't urge me to leave you or to turn back from you.
Where you go I will go, and where you stay I will stay. Your people
will be my people and/or God my God.
Where you die I will die, and there I will be buried.
May the Lord deal with me, be it every so severely, if anything but
death separates you and me."
Ruth 1: 16-17 (NIV)

"I have been looking for you!!!" my friend exclaimed.

When we met face to face for the first time in a long time, it was hard to tell her what happened. The truth is hard to swallow, let alone let back out into the world.

"Were you afraid of being judged?" she asked of my silence. *"Yes."* I answered.

Honesty is the way to retain friends. I was afraid of being rejected and judged. I assumed all of my friends would have an opinion that painted me in a bad light. I painted myself in a bad light. I wanted to rip that chapter of my life out and burn it. I didn't want to revisit it. It hurt. It was embarrassing. And it left scars. Nightmares. And dysfunction.

retain: to keep possession of.

From what we have learned about God's definition of friendship, we know that we have to hold onto our friendship with God first, so that He can filter our friendships through His standards. I believe that because we both seek God's standards, we are able to retain our friendship. When friendships become self-seeking, they either become dysfunctionally forced and flexed beyond their purpose, or they begin to fade and fall away. The only way to know the difference and step confidently into the next season with or without that person is to cling to God's truth, and obediently listen to it.

Ruth clung to Naomi because she felt the Lord's leading. "May the Lord deal with me…" That's when we cling. That's when we stick. That's when we know we've found a holy hug on this earth. Someone we can call upon and call out and visa versa, because we've found iron to sharpen iron. Friendship that is dependent on God is determined to last. Like David and Jonathan, though loyal to each other they could let go at anytime God called them away from each other. Like Ruth to Naomi, we can pull our friends a level up, and visa versa. Retaining friendships has less to do with where, what, and how …rather, Who, that friendship is rooted in.

The Water Weight

Maybe it's just because I've experienced the joy of pregnancy …but retain automatically triggers the synonymous phenomenon of "water weight." Long before my pregnant ankles actually started to swell, I thought they were huge. Unchecked information can cause our minds to create fictional circumstances. The sheer anticipation of outgrowing my socks made me over-analyze every line the elastic left on my ankles.

The truth was, my ankles never did swell. What of those lines, then? Long after kid number two, I started to notice that socks just left lines. Especially where the elastic was. Foot swelling or not. We do this in our friendships, don't we? I do. Easily cast off into the distance, in anticipation, of where our friendships are going.

If we're not careful to confide in God's truth concerning our friendships, we're libel to assign symptoms that aren't even there yet. It only takes one major hurt to activate the friendship filter. You know, the one where we qualify who is worthy of our time? Who's worth the risk? Who's capable of loyalty? We measure up the reputation of their past with their current situation and then project what we think their future holds …before we decide whether or not to keep them in our circle of friends. We "test period" each other. We look for the sock lines before the feet are even swelling.

Friendship is risky, because no one is perfect. We all come with hang-ups and baggage, and there's no telling what will happen when it all collides. When we're approaching it by and from God's standard and purpose, there's little guarantee except that we know God makes good of all things, all circumstances, and has a good plan for all of us.

I believe it's not up to us to decide who's allowed in the front door, up the stairs, down the hall, and into the friend room. That's God's call. His purpose. And our submission to it. Could we get hurt? Yep. Will it leave permanent sock lines? Maybe. But if we trust God's plan and purpose for our lives, that means we trust His plan and purpose for their lives.

"Where you go, I will go, and where you stay I will stay. Your people will be my people and your God my God." Ruth 1:16 (NIV)

I love the way the NIV Study Bible breaks Ruth's loyalty down: *"Her commitment to Naomi is complete, even though it holds no prospect for her but to share in Naomi's desolation."*

When is the last time we've fostered a friendship that had no personal gain in sight? A friend that we felt was God-placed in order for us to serve them, knowing there is nothing for us to gain but knowing that we are walking in His will as the extending arms of Christ's love.

Ruth's story ends with a hope and future that she could not have asked for or imagined when she simply decided to obey Him and remain loyal to her friend. One my closest friends has always told me in overwhelming moments of swirling responsibilities ..."just do the next thing." Yes. Ruth just did the next thing. She allowed God room to move ...and did He ever.

The Kick-Back

"A man of many companions may come to ruin, but there is a friend who sticks closer than a brother." Proverbs 18:24

Preconceived kick-backs from our friendships prevent us from retaining them. True friendship "loves at all times," in a forward and outward facing attitude of service and grace. Selfishness comes with a kick-back. The further we get into a friendship, the more we want to run when we're offended. We want to discount them as friends and disqualify them from deserving our time.

There's a trust-building stage in every friendship, and when that development is derailed, retention of that friendship should be brought into question. But who are we confiding in concerning the boundaries we place in our lives? How do we know if this friendship was for a season, which some are, or whether God is using iron to sharpen iron? Here are three good action-steps to take when considering whether to move forward in friendship.

1.Take a step back.

Sometimes the best way to honor our friends is to dedicate our hearts to prayer until the words we're meant to speak or the actions we're meant to take are clearly revealed by our Father. *"Whoever puts down another is not wise, but one who knows better keeps quiet." Proverbs 11:12 (VOICE paraphrase.)* **Resist the blame game, and choose not to be offended.**

"The loose tongue of the godless spreads destruction; the common sense of the godly preserves them." Proverbs 11:9 (Message)

I believe many of the problems we experience in friendship stem from smothering situations for immediate answers. We feel entitled to an explanation for our every hurt. Society encourages the right "air out truth," or subliminally address problems and offenses out on social media channels. But that's not the way to retain healthy friendships. We're not obligated to answer to the world, but we will face our Father.

"Seldom set foot in your neighbors house- too much of you, and they will hate you." Proverbs 25:17 (NIV)

Sometimes we can smother good friendships, because we are depending on them for their capability. Jesus is our rock. There is no substitute. I cringe at the number of times my mouth ran off and bent the ear of a friend beyond what they are meant to bear or absorb on my behalf. Not everyone is prepared or purposed to absorb all of our deepest hurts, nor are they equipped to bind them. Only Godly wisdom can soothe the sting of a faltering friendship.

The Voice paraphrases of Proverbs 25:17 reads, *"Don't visit your neighbor too often, or he will become tired of you and grow to hate you."* The Greek word for neighbor is this text is "friend, companion, fellow, another person." *(Strongs 7453)* God welcomes the pouring out of emotion that drips out of us when we're hurting, but we have to make sure our hearts are ready to obediently receive His wisdom in return.

Scripture promises us, *"Troublemakers start fights; gossips break friendships." Proverbs 16:28 (Message)* **A friend sets their ego aside to lift theirs up.** To honor our friends, even when they are wrong and owe us an apology, by extending grace to them that doesn't need to wait for it.

The Hebrew word for friend in context is 'alluwph, meaning "tame, docile." (Strongs 441) Conflict can take a perfectly healthy friendship and cause unnecessary sock lines. There is always a possibility that the offense we are envisioning is product of our imagination. But our lack of patience can cause us to jump all over our friends in offense.

Impatience will have us accusing others of manipulation, when they just ate a bad slice of pizza for lunch and bailed on our meet-up to barf. Honor friends and glorify God by giving Him room to illuminate what's really happening, and worth addressing. Don't create a hashtag for something that's not even trending yet.

2. Forgive forward.

Prayerfully lift up the friendship in question and ask God to illuminate both sides of the situation putting the entire friendship at risk. In a world consumed in text messages and social media, it's important to occasionally unplug and seek God's honest and right counsel. Forgiveness is an essential start, but a hard process to work through. Asking God to extend grace to our hearts, and theirs, sets us free from the blame game.

Imperfect people cannot master friendship perfectly. Only one Friend has the power of perfection. Jesus. He forgave immediately. We should aim to, as well. Although we're NOT Him, and it often won't happen immediately for us, we should immediately start working towards the process before seeds of bitterness sprout, bloom, and have babies all over the place. God taught me that forgiveness and reconciliation are not the same thing. It freed me to accept the process of forgiveness for what it is. Letting go. Giving it back to God so it doesn't hold me down.

Lifting it up over and over again so Christ by His authority to heal can heal my hurts and my friendships.

Being a mom to two daughters gives me a lot of opportunities to extend grace towards my own mom. As a child, I knew her as the one who told me "No," and rightly so. We fought through my teen years, which I now realize is normal. But I didn't know that back then. I can look back and let her off the hook, for what I didn't understand had to happen.

Friendship is the same way. We don't have to be forgiveness factories or no-boundaries doormats, but we can choose to forgive forward.

Forcing solutions strangles relationships. I want my daughters to extend grace for my parenting mistakes, and so I when my parents moved from down the street to across the country my motto to my broken hearted girls was this:

"I don't get it either. It hurts, and that's OK. When it hurts come to me and I will hug you and we'll hurt together. But just because we don't understand doesn't mean they don't love us any less, nor do we love them any less. Sometimes, we don't understand. And that's OK. God is good. God is bigger. And in time, we'll look back be able to see what we need to see."

When we apply this process of forgiving forward to our friends, we begin to see those people for who they are, and not what they do.

3. Find the fruit.

We're called to produce good fruit for the Lord. From Genesis to John, Scripture addresses "fruit." I believe we can find fruit in our friendships if we ask God for the ability to recognize it. When in a situation where we question what we are hearing and seeing with what our heart is screaming, find the fruit.

"A hot-tempered man stirs up dissension, but a patient man calms a quarrel." Proverbs 15:18

Dissension is a strong disagreement *(dictionary.com). James 1:9 states, "The brother in humble circumstances glory in his high position."(AMP)* Humble circumstances keep us humble. *"Everyone should be quick to listen, slow to speak and slow to become angry." (NIV notes)* Listen. Know your friend. *James 1:26, "If anyone who considers themselves religious leads them astray...")*

The comfort of association blinds us to treatment below God's standards. Removal from situations that are not fostering good fruit is crucial to attaining and retaining friendships. One rotten piece can spoil the whole fruit drawer. We're not being a good friend to someone by tolerating their bad behavior. The prayer is always for God to convict hearts to change, but we have to be willing to look in the mirror, and give Him space to work.

"He will die for lack of discipline, led astray by his own great folly." Proverbs 5:23 (NIV)

I'm not talking about lofting our own faith or relationship with God above anyone else's ...tooting our religious rule following horns or separating ourselves from people who don't align with us in every area of life. For example, I'm not going to discount a person as my friend because they gossip. But Scripture warns, the more we immerse ourselves in it, the more at risk we are of behaving that way. We can combat the negative by responding with something positive about the person who's character is being assaulted, or remove ourselves from gossip laden conversations.

A gossip-saturated friendship begs us to question a friend's authenticity and loyalty, based on how they treat and talk about everyone else. We should not be naive to think our names don't get a turn to roll out of their mouths in a negative light. Good friends hold each other accountable to higher standards. Instead of facing that difficult reality, I tolerated a gossip-saturated friendship for several years. One downfall seeped into many cracks. Heartfelt gifts were received with fake gratitude (*"Oh, my daughter will love this!"*), my time trod upon (*I was stood up for coffee dates and playdates with our daughters.*), and this friend became jealous of my other friendships. I wanted to break free, but thought good Christians were supposed to keep on forgiving.

When we get God's Truth twisted with what the world says, we start believing lies. Our enemy uses the Truth to confuse us. Deceit is his specialty. We risk mirroring the mistreatment we tolerate, and allowing it to trickle down into our other relationships. Because hurt people, hurt people.

I had aimed to be patient and listen, give of my time, and forgive. But in the process I started to catch myself gossiping. Seeds of bitterness grew as I started counting all the hours I dedicated to our friendship and expected her to reciprocate. I was manipulated and bullied, and this same friend's daughter sent mine home from school daily in tears.

Being a mom in that season made me stronger than I would have been had it just been my own heart at stake. It was time to stand up and shake off the lies that had accumulated and confront the fear of severing a friendship. I had not been a good friend by tolerating bad behavior. One Spring day, my daughter once again waded home from school though a puddle of hurt ...

"Let it go. It's OK. You are mine. I've got you. Just stand up, take the first step, run to me, and I'll heal you both. I'll show you who you are in Me."

Peace fell over us as I prayed to God. He started filling my minutes with other people. He guided me through difficult conversations. The good fruit of those friendships is not completely spoiled. We just don't always get it completely right …and it hurts.

Only God can change people. He tells us to pray for our enemies, and I did. I had to force my pen to write it on the pages of my journal most days, but I obeyed. I didn't talk about the whole thing much, just sat with God to heal. When the bulk of the bitterness passed, I began to share my story. After a year, He showed me exactly what to pray for. I wasn't the only one suffering. There were others. Moms and kids. And I knew then to begin praying for God to convict her heart, and her daughter's heart.

Not everyone is brave enough to speak out and speak up. But it's our job as Christians to turn around and help others who don't know how …and don't know Him.

We'll talk more about bullies and boundaries later in this book. But for now, the lesson is to embrace everyone where they are at. Cease knocking on door God has shut. The longer we wait to listen to Him, the harder the separation will be. I believe when we seek God daily in His Word, He will alert our nervous system like wildfire when we need to turn and run to Him.

Let's Pray …

Father,

Praise You for the way You scatter and allocate the minutes of our lives to touch others with Your love by it. The way You know us all so personally is amazing, and impossible to understand. As we go on *this journey to discover how to be friends with everyone, we want to do it Your way, and by Your will. Help us to remember that **"A man of many companions may come to ruin, but there is a friend who sticks closer than a brother." Proverbs 18:24***

Scripture warns us to watch our words and avoid gossip and slander, troublemakers and gossips that start fights and break friendships. Not all friendships will look the same way. Even Jesus had a circle of friends that He held closer than all the others. It's natural and God-intended that we guard our hearts, and choose those we expose our whole hearts to wisely. But remind us not to shut people out. Jesus was inclusive, and we should aim to be, too. Help us to avoid cliques, and to be ready and willing to extend an invite ...especially when it's out of our comfort zone.

Forgive us for holding grudges, and help us to forgive forward. Dissolve our tempers, and use us to defuse difficult matters. Help us to be disciplined, and to lead others to You. Search our hearts for any hidden agendas or opinions that do not align with Your Word and Your will.

In Jesus' Name,
Amen.

Chapter 10: Maintain

Growing and Fostering Friendships
(Free Your Friends ...Gain Forever Friendships.)

We are a society obsessed with control. Over how we look, what we eat, say, and who we count as our friends ...our "tribe."

Proverbs 14:22 states, "Do not those who plot evil go astray? But those who plan what is good find love and faithfulness."

Maintenance of our friendships brings God's all-inclusiveness down into view. Even through the attainment and retainment of friendships, if we are doing it right ...God's way ...we are planting seeds of friendships in lives along the way. Jesus had a select crew that He rolled with, but He didn't make everyone else feel rejected and unworthy just because He chose not to spend as much time with them as He did others.

The word "plan" is translated "devise" in the New American Standard Version of the Bible. The meaning behind the Hebrew for "devise" has a quiet connotation. (Strongs 2790) Planning and devising seem like words that infer a lot of action, movement, and voice. But the kind of planning that Proverbs 14:22 speaks of seems to be of a more quiet demeanor. A wiser tone.

By the time we've established friendships that need to be maintained, we've gathered a lot of common ground. There are a many reasons to keep this friendship going.

Hopefully, the friendships we've committed to maintain makes us feel like the people God says we are. They help us grow, and they let us go. These are friends that flow in and out of our lives as time goes on. The ones that we can relax around, trust, and we ourselves are loyal to. We all need loyal and trustworthy friends. They are hard to find. Once we've struck friendship gold, we want to maintain those relationships well.

maintain - to keep in existence or continuance; preserve, retain.

Since we've come this far in learning about how God defines friendship, we know that it happens in His time. As we learn how God instructs us to maintain friendships, keep these three things in mind:

1. Pray that our friendships glorify God.
2. Honor our friends by placing their needs above our own.
3. Foster the continued growth of our friendships by seeking Christ first.

Our time is limited. God is omnipotent. On earth, we must choose how to allocate our time, to whom and with whom. Even Jesus had to make that choice on earth. And there are some friendships that we will be led by Him to maintain more than others. Not through their fault or ours but by His will for our placement in each other lives.

We are loved immensely by our Father. He alone knows the unique purpose in our individual make-up. **Only the Father can bring together for His Kingdom purposes those He ordained for them.** We don't know that about each other …unless He reveals it.

Another version of *Proverbs 14:22 reads, "Don't those who work evil stray from the truth? Those who plan goodness experience unfailing love and faithfulness." (VOICE)*

When we allow God to filter imperfections through His perspective, we will be left with friendships that are meant to weave in and out of our lives in His perfect time.

The Mediator

Christians talk a lot about God-placed friends, but the apostle Paul gave us some amazing models for maintaining friendships for His glory.

Evidence of grace can be found in the book of Philemon, a single chapter tucked into the rest of Paul's letters. Believer to believer, he writes to Philemon concerning an escaped slave who had stolen from him. Onesimus had become a Christian.

God works in, out, and through human imperfection. He is compassionate towards us, using every life, missteps and triumphs, for His glory.

It made a difference to Philemon that Onesimus had become a Christian. Paul smartly reminded him in the beginning of the letter of his own humble stature. Jesus called him straight out of persecuting Christians to follow Him. *(1 Corinthians 15:9)*

"If he has done you any wrong or owes you anything, charge it to me." Philemon 18

That's what Jesus did for us on the cross. *(Galatians 3:13)* The story of Paul and Philemon extends a glimpse of our compassionate Father, wanting every heart to hear the gospel. That's why He sent Jesus. We all get stuck in the ways of society. In worldly ways. God warns us to have nothing to do with it *(2Timothy 3:5)*, but He doesn't abandon us for our human imperfection.

God's not after perfection, but surely isn't justifying our sin either. That's why we need Jesus for salvation.

Don't put it past Him to work a miracle through a fallen situation. To restore life to a dead place. To save a heart that the rest of us deem unworthy and less than.

"Perhaps the reason he was separated from you for a little while was that you might have him back for good- no longer as a slave, but better than a slave, as a dear brother." Philemon 15

"I appeal to you for my son ...who became my son while I was in chains," Paul speaks of his friend. We often find friends in hard seasons.

A single friendship cannot uphold constant alignment on every issue. God slowly builds layers into friendship over time. If we force our views and opinions on our friends, rather than loving each other for who we are and where we're at in life, the friendship will fail. Space to breathe allows us to see through the extended arms of friends..

It's that base level of unbreakable trust. *"I am sending him- who is my very heart- back to you."*

The connections we make in this life are never coincidental, because our God - who created every person -is not a God of coincidence. He's a God of purpose. Each friendship has a purpose, we may or may not know until we make a connection.

Paul's obedience to keep a Christ-like open heart to people allowed him to understand friendships that could only be God-ordained. In a world pre-"mutual" friend exposed by social media, he brought these three friends together for a purpose they could not have known …a meeting they could not have arranged.

In a way, Paul was the mediator in this situation, begging both sides to see the good in each other. To look past mistakes and titles, even the law, and towards forgiveness. That is what Jesus did for us on the cross.

The Tentmakers

"Greet Priscilla and Aquila, my fellow workers in Christ Jesus. They risk their lives for me. Not only I but all the churches of the Gentiles are grateful to them. Greet also the church that meets at their house." Romans 16: 2-5a (NIV)

I love that Priscilla is listed before her husband, Aquila, because it shows us a piece of God's character. None are exempt from taking up our cross and leading for the Lord.

Paul showed up at Priscilla and Aquila's house to learn they were tentmakers just like he. He extended his stay beyond the customary length of time.

"There he found a Jew named Aquila, a native on Pontus, who had recently come from Italy wit his wife, Priscilla, because Claudius had ordered all the Jews to depart from Rome. Paul approached them, and because he worked at the same trade, he stayed with them and worked with them (for they were teenagers by trade)" Acts 18:2-3 NIV

In the Old Testament, expanding tents was sometimes used to convey a forthcoming blessing, especially for a family wishing to have children.

"Enlarge the place of your tent, stretch your tent curtains wide, do not hold back; lengthen your cords, strengthen your stakes."
Isaiah 54:2 (NIV)

They would naturally have to expand their tent. Paul, as he proceeds to expand the church family, finds a family in the same business. And by the time he leaves them, they are having church in their house. God used their very profession to bring them together, proving that we can honor God in any profession He places us in.

These friends risked their lives for Paul, proclaimed the Gospel truth and grew the church with Paul. God connected them on so many levels, that their friendship permeated any distance or time in between visits. An experience, and an extended stay, that forever marked their hearts as friends on a mission for Christ.

By following His will for their lives, as He does for ours, Christ provided an extension of His loving and encouraging arms through their friendship.

Friendships form the church. It's not a building we are in or the denomination of we claim …it's the Christ fed and Christ led friendships of open armed inclusion. Our willingness to being friends with everyone extends Christ's friendship to all that cross our path …in His time.

The Wise Buddies

Sometimes God places friends in our lives that are a decade behind or ahead of us. Thinking back to school days, I would have never consulted a First Grader when I was a Junior in High School. Nor would I have had thought a thirty-year-old would have anything relevant to say to me when I was eighteen. But when a friend of mine recently expressed her search for a mentor or a friend her age, I felt God leading me to tell her that age doesn't matter. It usually means, I was supposed to apply the same statement to my own life.

Which reminded me of one of my favorite mentor/mentee friendships from the New Testament. Paul and Timothy.

Paul encouraged Timothy to *" ...hold to the things that you have learned and of which you are convinced, known from whom you learned [them]" -2Timothy 3:14.*

These friends came from similar faith, but different faith experiences.

"Timothy learned his faith from observing his mother, Eunice... who in turn learned her faith from observing her mother, Lois. (2Timothy 1:5).

In 2 Timothy 3:15, Paul reminds Timothy of his salvation in Jesus Christ, and the knowledge and treasures of the Word that have been stored in his heart since childhood.

"All Scripture is God-breathed and is useful for teaching, rebuking, correcting, and training in righteousness (NIV), So that the man of God may be complete an proficient, well fitted and thoroughly equipped for every good work." -2Timoty 3:16-17 (AMP)

Scripture is ageless, and although we do maintain friendships based on the commonality of the generation we grew up in, there is much wisdom to gain by absorbing the wisdom of those who have gone before us, and come up behind us. The body of Christ was designed to function together regardless of color, ethnicity, background ...and age.

Let's Pray ...

Father,

Praise You for the perfect way You maintain Your relationship with all of us simultaneously. We can barely manage one at a time! You're love is amazing. It's huge. It's inclusive. Help us to be those that "plan what is good," as Proverbs 14:22 says, so that we "find love and faithfulness."

The story of Paul and Onesimus reflects the restoring love You have for us. Help us to be humble and willing to trade our agendas for Yours. To focus on Your word before our rules. Jesus died to make us right with You. His sacrifice on the cross paid for what we owe because of sin. Let us grip that grace so tight that it flows out of us wherever we go, and to whomever we talk to. May our hearts beam with the inclusive grace and love and hope of our Savior, attracting questions and opportunities to share the Gospel and make new friends.

Help us to trust Your will, as Paul did. To put our own agendas and goals aside for what You map out for us, day by day. Allow our hearts to be molded so much like Christ's that we are able to love people like they are our very own brothers or sisters or children or mothers or fathers! Teach us to love that big. Allow us to **" ...hold to the things that you have learned and of which you are convinced, known from whom you learned [them]" -2Timothy 3:14.** *And may the Holy Spirit constantly remind us that* **"All Scripture is God-breathed and is useful for teaching, rebuking, correcting, and training in righteousness (NIV), So that the man of God may be complete an proficient, well fitted and thoroughly equipped for every good work." -2Timothy 3:16-17 (AMP)**

We pray, today, for God-placed friends to become evident. Open our eyes and reveal Your plan to us minute by minute, and day by day. As we learn to abide in You, we will better understand Your definition of and purpose for friendship. It's simply not about us, but we are set to that default. Align our hearts and minds to Your love and Your Word and Your will.

In Jesus' Name,
Amen.

Section Four

But What Happens When …

Chapter 11
The Forgiveness Factory

Forgiveness vs. Reconciliation
Barricades vs. Boundaries

How do we handle conflict in our friendships? What do we do when they are derailed by dishonesty, disloyalty, abuse or loss of trust? Relationships remain imperfect because humanity is incapable of selfless love.

Due to the fall in the garden of Eden, we are continually cursed with sin, preventing flawless communication with each other. Only one pair of feet walked the earth in perfect obedience to God. Jesus came out of compassion for us. His love grants forgiveness and love. Through Him we can find victory in our relationships, despite imperfect behavior.

"For He Himself is our peace, who has made the two groups one and has destroyed the barrier, the dividing wall of hostility."
Ephesians 2:14 (NIV)

Before Jesus walked the earth, the Jewish people were the chosen people of God. The Gentiles were looked down upon. Equate it to how society still throws people into categories deemed unworthy.

The Gentiles were made to feel as if they did not deserve forgiveness for their sins.

God forgives everyone, we are all created equal. But in our less than worthy hearts, it's hard to reconcile the fact that our fate could be equal to the sex-traffickers, murderers, and so-called "scum" of society. Those in jail and those in church every Sunday.

Christ coming to save all people was a shocking concept to God's chosen people. Jew *and* Gentile? It was as nonsensical to them as it is for us to consider ourselves equal to those guilty of horrible acts on death row.

1Peter 2:9 says, "But you are a chosen people, a royal priesthood, a holy nation, God's special possession, that you may declare the praises of him who called you out of darkness into his wonderful light." (NIV)

"Priest" comes from a root word meaning *"to serve."* We are all called to serve. We can each insert our names into the *"you"* of 1Peter 2:9 and know that it's for us. Meg, you are a chosen person, a royal priest, a holy nation, God's special possession. I am, you are, and they are. We ALL are.

"That I may declare the praises of him who called me out of the darkness into his wonderful light." There isn't a hierarchy of ministry. We don't have to be pastors to be qualified to *"declare the praises of Him who call us out of the darkness."* Christ meets us where we are at, and asks that we minister to those within our reach.

Jesus, our Peace, is the solution to all conflict. He came to join together what we divide. When choose to fight and declare a winner, we lose. He loves us all. He came for us all. Jew and Gentile. Victim and bully. Some might yearn for the blessing we fail to be grateful for. We could be the very oppression in someone's life that we have suffered from in our own. Healing comes from helping others. Let's look in the mirror ...turn around ...and face out.

The very definition of 'struggle' is *"to contend with an adversary or opposing force."* We are set to a defensive default, but created to love.

"And now these three remain: faith, hope and love. But the greatest of these is love." 1 Corinthians 13:13

Jesus taught that this was the most important command. The NIV Notes on this verse say that *"Jesus' teaching united his followers around love."* Unity is the opposite of struggling opposition. There's nothing we can do to force our relationships to work. But we can focus on Love.

"The most important one," answered Jesus, "is this:
'Hear, O Israel: The Lord our God, the Lord is one. Love the Lord your God with all your heart and with all your soul and with all your mind and with all your strength.'
The second is this:
"'Love your neighbor as yourself.' There is no commandment greater than these." -Mark 12:29-31

The door may close on unhealthy relationships. I believe any fallout can be mended with Love, but potential reconciliation is often ruined by pride. When we ask God to help us recognize the hardships that we bring into our relationships, our hearts can begin to grow out of that conviction. Prayer and time in God's word can give us direction on the path to constructing new bridges where old ones have been burned.

God is love. We can cry out to Him in pain when our relationships are hard and hurting. He commands us to love, but we cannot accomplish it without His grace. Having compassion for the imperfect people we are allows forgiveness to flow easier, and bids reconciliation a better chance. Christ's example shows us how to find a way to mend our struggles with love.

The journey of forgiveness will not always end in reconciliation here on this earth. Conflict is messy, full of pride, offense and defense, and genuine hurt. Misunderstanding and ignorance run rampant in our messes. We have a very real enemy that likes to fan the flames of a fight. If we're not careful, careless choices will create division.

Our "frenemies" are beloved children of God, too. In the midst of conflict, we can choose to see friendship as an opportunity to grow, and grow others. To serve, and be served. To love, and be loved. Its messy. It hurts. It requires pride to sit the bench. But we can walk in friendships the way God intended, if we purposely choose to pursue what He says about it. Especially about resolving conflict, and pursuing reconciliation at the end of forgiveness road.

Seek God's standard. Follow Christ's lead.

The Game of Telephone

Chatter can have a devastating effect on friendship, because it's so closely linked with trust. The book of Proverbs is full of wisdom, and the topic of *"chatter"* is prevalent. I love that we can run to God for advice on this relevant topic, to find His guiding hand in ancient Scripture weaving living Truth through our lives right now. Truly when we seek Him, we will find Him.

"He who covers over an offense promotes love, but whoever repeats the matter separates close friends." Proverbs 17: 9 (NIV)

When determining whether to direct our forgiveness towards reconciliation, it's important to note the frequency offenses. A first-time offense can often be forgiven quickly, with reconciliation immediately following. Perhaps we ask a friend to forgo downloading someone's backstory before we get to know them ourselves. They oblige, the behavior stops, and we move on with a new level of respect for each other.

If the behavior is not addressed, and they continue to disregard our request, it may be time to remove ourselves from those conversations, completely. Choose who your support system is wisely.

Looking back at some of the first time offenses in my friendship highlight reel, I would have chosen to guard my heart more cautiously. Some patterns cannot be broken simply by our tolerance to endure them. We're not doing our friends any favors by sitting in the wreckage of their dysfunction, and visa versa.

Proverbs 17:9 assures us that the frequency of the offense matters, but even first-time offenses can be filtered through God's wisdom. Proverbs 10:12 states, **"Hatred stirs up dissension, but love covers over all wrongs."** The NIV Study Bible Notes define *"covers all wrongs,"* as *"promotes forgiveness."* We are not fostering healthy forgiveness when we approve of and tolerate dysfunction in our relationships. That sends a girl like me, who's afraid of confrontation more than the proverbial monster in my closet, into a panic.

"Can't you just handle this, God?" I whine.

"Can you throw a blanket of protection over me and sweep me out of this situation? Make it disappear? Make them disappear? That would be great. Thank you. Amen."

"Remember this: Whoever turns a sinner from the error of his way will save him from death and cover a multitude of sins." James 5:20 (NIV)

Time and again He gently reminds me that it's not about me.

And honestly, I cringe when He says that to me, because I know the process of going deep with people in His honor is painful and hard. It means that He's about to grow me in the right direction, which makes me want to run the other way. Why? Because growing pains hurt!

The NIV notes on James 5:20 convict me to the core: *"The sins of the wanderer will be forgiven by God."*

When I wander away from a situation in disobedience, my soul goes crazy. It screams at me to turn around and run to God. But can I be honest? Sometimes, I freeze. I can't get there. I want to be obedient but my feet and my mouth won't operate in tune with God's Truth. Guilt, shame, and fear wash over me and I disqualify myself. But thankfully, it's not about me. It's about Jesus.

There's nothing *I* can do to get my feet moving and my mouth cooperating, but He can. And that's it. It's His power and authority working through me that glorify God and accomplish His will in my life. The release of forgiveness puts reconciliation in His hands.

It's obeying His Word, and letting the chips fall where they may … not freezing in fear of what will happen. He has pressed upon my heart not to write the ending before He's revealed it.

Being pushed around in one particular friendship helped me understand the process of obedience and submission. I forgave and forgave, but kept getting mulled over. Disregarded. Disrespected. Hurt. My daughter suffered through her own battle simultaneously, as we kept finding ways to forgive offenses and fend off hurt from a mother/daughter friendship duel bullying nightmare.

One day, as we both let fresh tears of pure situational exhaustion fall to the kitchen floor, I felt Jesus' peace wash over me, and release me from the line of fire. *"That's enough. Now let me."* I knew in that moment that the road of forgiveness we were on with our friends would not end in reconciliation.

"Above all, love each other deeply, because love covers over a multitude of sins." 1 Peter 4:8 (NIV)

Each offense against us, when aligned with His Truth, will be worked out in love. But be prepared. Sometimes that requires a season of isolation, shifting, and *'pray for your enemy'* praying. When we seek Him first in these seasons, we emerge changed and equipped to be His compassionate hands of love as we turn to help others going through what we just came out of.

Can we forgive every offense? Yes. We're called to love and love never fails to forgive. Sometimes immediately, sometimes eventually, sometimes it's a lifelong process …but yes. Will forgiveness always lead to reconciliation? No. Sometimes we just blow it with people.

We are subject to the imperfection of this world and the sinful nature in every one of us. Reconciliation will not always be realistic. And we have to be ready and willing to walk away. Or, to mourn the loss and move on with the aim to be a better friend in the future. He is faithful to let us anchor in safe harbors, every-time …but sometimes, without the ones we want with us.

We have a very real enemy looking to trip us up, and we can't allow our hearts to get caught up in the one *"who plots evil with deceit in his heart- he always stirs up dissension." Proverbs 6:14 (NIV)* We pit ourselves against each other, which plays right into his hands. Maybe the best way to honor someone is by stepping back, or speaking up.

Scripture tells us to go to our friends when their behavior is out of line. Friends know each other well, and should be able to go to each other one on one to address a hurt or concern. But if that doesn't work, we're to go to them with another friend, possibly a small group. Matthew 18:15-17 addresses what to do about these behaviors in the church. But I believe it's applicable to close friends, as well.

"If your brother or sister sins, go and point out their fault, just between the two of you. If they listen to you, you have won them over. But if they will not listen, take one or two others along, so that 'every matter may be established by the testimony of two or three witnesses.' If they still refuse to listen, tell into the church; and if they refuse to listen even to the church, treat them as you would a pagan or a tax collector." Matthew 18:15-17 NIV

I'm reminded of the old distance runner mantra … *"Lead, follow, or get out of the way."* We are to let nothing get in the way of Christ's call on our lives, and to admonish each other along the way. Let's not forget, God places people in our lives purposefully. So often, our pride prevents us from hearing people that are truly trying to help us grow. Or, we are afraid to offend our friends so we instead focus on *only* the good. Good friends love us when we are hard to love. They aren't afraid to take a risk and puncture an uncomfortable situation or call us out when we're wrong.

The Criss-Crossed Woman

Forgiveness is hard. It's not always about us, and our defense. With a servant attitude of love, there is a job for us to do. God is not a God of coincidence, misplaced minutes, or wasted time. Every mistake and misstep is an opportunity for growth.

Mary got it. I picture her criss-cross applesauce on the floor at Jesus' feet, while her sister Martha ran frantically around the house. We do this, don't we? Run around trying to fix-up and clean-up …when nothing we can do will accomplish the healing we are after.

"Mary, who sat at the Lord's feet, listening to Him." Luke 10:23 (NIV) Jesus doesn't love us less when we rush around, but He does ache for us to sit with Him.

Both the sister that rushed around and the sister that sat called on Jesus when their brother was ill to the point of death. Repeated twice in the eleventh chapter of John, each sister calls upon Him with the same faith.

"'Lord,' Martha said to Jesus, 'if you had been here, my brother would not have died.'" John 11:21 (NIV)

"When Mary reached the place where Jesus was and saw him, she fell at his feet and said, 'Lord, if you had been here, my brother would not have died.'" John 11:32

Though Martha rushed around frantically, she repeated what she knew to be true, *"I know that even now God will give you whatever you ask." (v22)*

She ran to get Mary, who found Jesus' feet and hit her knees.

Through their story we can see the character of our great God. Jesus wept for them. Not one over the other. Jesus was human. He get's us. He compassionately embraces us in the pain that He, Himself, felt to the core. And He raised their brother from the dead.

Jesus came to bring life. We should want to see a change in a friend that we have fallen out with, and crave the conviction to change in our own. If we don't know we're hurting someone, or they don't' know they are hurting us, how can either side truly heal?

Run to Him in obedience. He will resurrect the dead things in our lives, the forgiveness that we cannot muster, and sometimes the reconciliation that we never thought possible. No matter how we run to him …frantically repeating His Truth like Martha, or hitting our knees in an ugly cry like Mary, He will meet us there. He will heal us, grow, and continue to love us. If only, we could embrace differences and difficulties in each other as He does ours.

Healthy Boundaries

"Even my best friend, the one I trusted completely ...has turned agains me. " Psalm 41:9

For someone to have a seat of honor at the king's table signals an important relationship. This verse most likely speaks of King David's Prime Minister and friend, *"whose advice he relied much upon in dealing with his enemies."* Suffering, in Old Testament Biblical times, might have signaled friends to disassociate themselves rather than risk a similar punishment. Jesus, however, loved His friends, and loves us, regardless of what they, and we, deserve. There is never a reason to permanently lock someone out of the friend room. But there are potentially unhealthy seasons of friendship, and boundaries to love them within. [16]

Guarding our hearts God's way is essential in forming and maintaining healthy friendships that glorify God and spread the love of Jesus.

Dr. Henry Cloud and Dr. John Townsend authored, "Boundaries," which weaves Christian principles into the psychological need for boundaries in our lives. *"Boundaries are not walls,"* they state, *"The Bible does not say that we are to be 'walled off' from others; in fact, it says that we are to be 'one' with them (John 17:11).*

In the process of writing this book on being friends with everyone, I realized that I had little boundaries with anyone. A tour back into

---

[16] "10 Types of Harmful Friends and How to Set Boundaries with Each," https://www.ibelieve.com/slideshows/10-harmful-types-of-friends-and-how-to-set-boundaries-with-each.html

some of the friendships that have derailed in my life popped up as proof of my lack in this area. I had a tendency to be instantly forgiving and extremely compliant on the surface, even if I was actually annoyed and aggravated. Trying to be a good "friend" in that way caused me to eventually get tired of my self-imposed 'door-mat' status and simply close the door.

Learning about healthy boundaries has allowed me be friends with everyone, authentically. Even the difficult ones that I have learned to hold wisely at arm's length. It turns out, much of my fear of conflict resulted from an absolute absence of boundaries.

"I am no longer in the world; and yet they themselves are in the world, and I come to You. Holy Father, keep them in Your name, the name which You have given Me, that they may be one even as We are." John 17:11 NASB

We are better together when we honor the person God created us to be. Boundaries go beyond friendships. Trying to be someone we were never intended to be can create unauthentic relationships, along with conflict and misunderstanding within ourselves and with our friends.

"In the same way he gave us his 'likeness' (Gen. 1:26), he gave us personal responsibility within limits. He wants us to 'rule over' the earth and to be responsible stewards over the life he has given us. To do that, we need to develop boundaries like God's." -Boundaries, Dr. Henry Cloud and Dr. John Townsend

Looking further into John 17:11, I discovered that the original Greek translation for *"one"* is ...*"one." (Strongs 1520)* The NIV Study Bible Notes state, *"Here the unity is already given, not something to be achieved."* Constructing healthy boundaries is getting to root of our role in maintaining the unity that already exists by Christ's victory on the cross. We cannot function in unity a part from Christ. Things like comparison, envy, pride, and a slew of other character faults grafted into the human experience along with sin prevent us from accomplishing unity on our own. But in Christ, we can find peace …and healthy boundaries …in order to embrace our originality, and accomplish authentic friendships.

Here is an excerpt from Boundaries, by Dr. Henry Cloud and Dr. John Townsend, regarding 'Boundaries and Your Friends:"

"Choice and commitment are elements of a good friendship. We do need more than fair-weather friends. However, Scripture teaches us that we can't depend on commitment or sheer willpower, for they will always let us down. Paul cried out that he did what he didn't want to do, and he didn't do what he wanted to do (Romans 7:19). He was stuck. We all experience the same conflict. Even when we commit to a loving friendship, bad things happen. We let our friends down. Feelings go sour. Simply white-knuckling it won't reestablish the relationship.

We can solve our dilemma the same way Paul solved his: 'Therefore, there is now no condemnation for those who are in Christ Jesus (Rom 8;1). The answer is being 'in Christ Jesus' - in other words, in relationship with Christ, both vertically and horizontally. As we stay filled up with the grace to hang in there and fight out the boundary conflicts that arise. Without this external source of connections, we're doomed to an empty willpower that ultimately fails or makes us think we're omnipotent.

The Bible teaches that all commitment is based on a loving relationship. Being loved leads to commitment and willful decision making- not the reverse."

Boundaries with Bullies

Psychology Today states that, <u>"Bullies are not born, they are made."</u> Are we paying attention to our adult relationships, in order to cue the generations coming up behind us on how to behave, and what not to allow? When we accept treatment from a bully, we are unfortunately sending a message to our children that this behavior is not only acceptable, but to be tolerated. A recent article challenged parents to *"model what they want the children to do."*[17]

When the plight to 'forgive and focus on the good' has turned us in to a friend yo-yo, our hearts are undoubtedly being pushed around. "Bullying is a distinctive pattern of harming and humiliating others, specifically those who are in some way smaller, weaker, younger, or in anyway more vulnerable than the bully." [18]

The Bible reminds us to pray for our enemies *(Luke 6:27-28),* and to live peaceably with all *(Romans 12:18-19).* Set healthy boundaries that restrict access to these types of friends, but remember that the purpose of all relationships is to foster the love of Christ. God's protective hand will defend us. *(If, by setting boundaries, we feel threatened in a dangerous way, Dr. Susan Bilai M.D. advises, "If you're dealing with a bully of that degree, you need the help of a professional when it comes to setting boundaries and keeping yourself safe.")* [19][20]

"Your too Sensitive."

I've been accused of it often, and have even noticed it myself. Noticing things that other people don't pick up on. We aren't always privy to why we are the way we are. When that happens, I implore you from personal experience to hold on tight to the Scriptures that

---

[17] https://www.psychologytoday.com/us/blog/acquired-spontaneity/201206/more-about-bullying

[18] https://www.psychologytoday.com/us/basics/bullying

[19] "10 Types of Harmful Friends and How to Set Boundaries with Each," Meg Bucher

[20] https://www.psychologytoday.com/us/blog/prescriptions-life/201304/if-you-set-boundary-expect-deal-anger

assure us that God goes before us and defends us. I know what it's like to have my heart's good intentions go misunderstood. To be falsely accused and put into unfair positions. I've had my character questioned by some of those closest to me, been taken advantaged of and even abused. It's not OK …but I am.

In the process of writing this book, I felt it was time for a mental check up. There were certain circumstances and dead-end arguments that kept cropping up in my life cyclicly. In writing a book called *'Friends with Everyone,'* I felt it wise to seek a Christian counselor to make sure I was on the right track with my own personal relationships, before advising others on how to navigate theirs.

"I think you might be this type of person," my counselor hinted after the first few visits. *"Look into this and let me know what you think."*

Through her counsel, Christ broke through a stronghold I didn't know existed. I'm an HSP. A Highly Sensitive Person. Every memory came flooding back and re-categorized itself, emboldening me to embrace who I was like I never had before. 20% of the world carries this genetic personality trait, making it too big of a number of people for it to be a dysfunction. Most HSP's are introverts. Only 30% are extroverted. You guessed it. I'm a 30% of a 20%. [21]There's much I'd love to share with you about life as an HSP, and will do so in the pages of my next book, *Surface.*

Seek wisdom and revelation. I was able to embrace boundaries on a whole new level, understanding why my intuition was always on overdrive. (Visit **hsperson.com** for more information about HSP.) Don't give up on yourself. Continue to seek God's wisdom. He will blow you away, and give you the ability to bless others with your friendship.

---

[21] https://hsperson.com

"It's what you did, not who you are," I bravely repeated to a friend that no longer had the permission wound or walk all over me. *"You have to separate the two."* I had, and it felt amazing. I screeched in celebration on the drive home. Conflict can be messy. Boundaries are hard to construct in love. Truth sets us free. Be open to criticism from good friends. It can be the healing hand that saves us from making terrible and painful mistakes. But be wise not to let other people label their poor behavior as something you did or earned because of who you are. Have courage. Be kind. Be assertive and strong in the face of fear. And above all, ***"Seek first his kingdom and his righteousness, and all these things will be given to you as well." Matthew 6:33 NIV***

Jesus addressed our provisional worry in Matthew 6:25-34 God not only provides for our physical needs, but He is faithful to provide for us emotionally and spiritually. In a way that we could never muster the appropriate words to pray for, He is there for us. Perfect Love. Human conflict and the hurt that results can be some of the most devastating wounds to endure. He is close to us through it all, and tells us not to worry. Lift it up to Him, keep seeking, and continue to obey His directive steps.

You were made for such a time as this (Esther 3:14) …and friends like these.

Let's Pray …

Father,

Praise You for Love. We don't understand it. The little that we do understand we so often don't execute correctly. Yet You remind us, ***"And now these three remain: faith, hope and love. But the greatest of these is love." 1 Corinthians 13:13*** *As we reflect on the placement of others in our lives and us in theirs, help us to pray these truths into our memories and to write them on our hearts in such a way that we live them out daily:*

"The most important one," answered Jesus, "is this:
'Hear, O Israel: The Lord our God, the Lord is one. Love the Lord
your God with all your heart and with all your soul and with all
your mind and with all your strength.'
The second is this:
'Love your neighbor as yourself.' There is no commandment
greater than these."
Mark 12:29-31

You have to come first. But so often, Father, You don't. Forgive us for
placing anything above or before You. Help us to learn how to love a
little more each day as You perfect our hearts to holiness throughout
our entire lives. Give us hearts like Jesus,' that are able to serve
others and love others as He did on earth, and does for all of us in
His pursuit of our hearts.

Help us to turn from from our dysfunction, and so lead others to
*Your love, as we apply the words of Your truth: **"Remember this:***
Whoever turns a sinner from the error of his way will save him
from death and cover a multitude of sins." James 5:20 (NIV)
Allow us to endure injustice and hardship at the expense of others
*because You say, **Above all, love each other deeply, because love***
covers over a multitude of sins." 1 Peter 4:8 (NIV)

We learned from Mary to sit with You. And we learned that we are
going to be slighted in this life, but that nothing is out of Your reach
or line of sight. Your love for us is greater than anything we will
*endure here on earth. **Proverbs 9:10** reminds, **"The fear of the Lord***
is the beginning of wisdom, and knowledge of the Holy One is
understanding."

Praise You for Jesus' example on this earth. We know that You are
purposeful in the plan that You have for our lives, and for the people
that you place in it. We are not always going to get along with
everyone. Not always going to execute our behavior in Christ-like

fashion. Help alleviate the shame of our imperfection, and help us to extend that grace to others.

Christ came to forgive us for every misbehavior He knew that we would choose to suffer by. Imperfect people dealing with imperfect people can get a little messy down on earth. We ask for You to cover us in Your grace, and convict our hearts to change. Forgive us for letting the sharp edges of our sensitivities take over conversations, and the anxieties of our minds to cloud our judgement. Help us to see others through Your eyes, as souls that You love just as much as You love ours.

Bless our hearts to soften towards others, yet protect us from deceptive motives. When there is a relationship that you wish us to walk away from, help us to hear a clear word from You. Bless our friendships to be godly and God-centered. Show us, by illuminating Your Word and blessing us with Your presence, how to be more like Jesus, how to love as He spoke, and You command.

In Jesus' Name,
Amen.

Chapter 12

Wounding Words and Distorted Thoughts

Gossip is hard ...to resist ...to deflect ...to avoid. If we want to be good friends, we have to check our emotions through a prayerful filter before we react out loud.

Proverbs 14:16-17 states, "A wise man fears the Lord and shuns evil, but a fool is hotheaded and reckless. A quick-tempered man does foolish things, and crafty man is heated." (NIV)

Gossip is reckless. And man is crafty. We have to watch our tongues lest they run away from us. In 1 Kings 22:23, we find a group of prophets who are caught in lies. ***"So now the Lord has put a lying spirit in the mouths of all these prophets of yours. The Lord has decreed disaster for you."*** (NIV) The NIV Study Bible notes explain what was happening here:

"Some view the lying spirit as Satan or one of his agents. Others have suggested a spirit of God who undertakes the task of a lying spirit of God (but see 1 Samuel 15:29). Still others understand the lying spirit as a symbolic picture of the power of the lie. The Lord had given the 400 prophets over to the power of the lie because they did not love the truth and had chosen to speak out of their own hearts."

When we are in denial, we can spin a web of falsities that we begin to believe and speak as actual truths. If we are embarrassed about our reaction or behavior, we can retell the story in a way that doesn't make it seem as bad as it was. Stick to the honest truth when retelling a story. Even the little white lies of detail are still lies. They are just as destructive.

"The Lord who rules over all says to the people of Jerusalem:
"Do not listen to what
those prophets are saying to you.
They are filling you with false hopes.
They are reporting visions of their own imaginations,
not something the Lord has given them to say." Jeremiah 23:16
(NET)

These prophets were making up stuff that God said! Preposterous! But prevalent! Both back in Biblical times, and now. Any good preacher, writer, or speaker, will honor anyone who lines what they have to say up to God's Word and finds an error. We are human! Line up every Biblical truth preached from a pulpit, book, a living room, a TV screen, or a podcast.

Gossip is rooted in lies, or twisted truths. What begins as an honest conversation can become an undermined intention to throw someone under the bus. It's deceitful, slippery slope, and one of the devil's favorite tools. Lying is his specialty, and he aims to *"kill, steal, and destroy." (John 10:10)* A stolen, destroyed, or annihilated reputation can emotionally destroy a person. We are to have nothing to do with those conversations *(2 Timothy 3:5b).*[22]

---

[22] "A Prayer for Those Caught in the Gossip Trap," https://www.crosswalk.com/devotionals/your-daily-prayer/a-prayer-for-those-caught-in-the-gossip-trap-your-daily-prayer-january-19-2018.html

Be careful not to believe everything that comes out of people's mouths or appears on their social media feeds. Behind every highlight reel is a real struggle. In every conversation, the temptation to twist the truth is present. Seeking God daily helps alert us to what is true and what is not true …and what is not worth stewing over. Leave reckless conversations. Change the subject when emotions flare or left-over bitterness rears it's ugly head. We are easily tempted in those situations to believe lies of comparison and jealousy, and to dishonor another person's character with our speech …or even with our nodding along.

The Friendly Chatter

"If only I knew where to find him;
* if only I could go to his dwelling!" Job 23:3 (NIV)*

With every bullying prevention week that goes by, we're all reminded of how cruel kids can be. It seems to be getting worse and worse. Tender hearts are broken everyday on the playground. Personalities are wounded in the hallways. God created each person with unique care. But the beautiful way we began is now stripped down and shoved into proverbial lockers.

What's more leveling than how bad bullying has gotten? The fact that they get it from us.

Kids mimic what they see and speak what they hear. They are listening, and the tone we amplify is reflected in their classroom and out on the practice fields.

In today's verse, Job is responding to some friends that have come to "advise" him. His life had fallen a part, and they remained convinced that he'd gotten what he'd deserved, a just punishment for sin.

"Job replied:
"I'm not letting up—I'm standing my ground.

My complaint is legitimate.
God has no right to treat me like this—
it isn't fair!
If I knew where on earth to find him,
I'd go straight to him.
I'd lay my case before him face-to-face,
give him all my arguments firsthand.
I'd find out exactly what he's thinking,
discover what's going on in his head.
Do you think he'd dismiss me or bully me?
No, he'd take me seriously.
He'd see a straight-living man standing before him;
my Judge would acquit me for good of all charges." Job 23:1-7
(MSG)

Job longs to for an audience with God to ask Him "why." He's at a loss as to why God has abandoned and failed to defend Him in the way Job wants Him to. His friends are maddening him with their reasoning for his suffering.

How terrible is it to stand helpless while our character is compromised?

For a time Job felt hopeless. He wrestled with God about the unfairness of it all. We, too can wrestle like Job.

Jesus intercedes for us, loves us, and defends us when we cannot. His tender heart understands the ridicule of this world because He endured it, Himself.

What Job longed for …a way to reach out to God …we have. Every heart that has accepted Christ has His very Spirit living in it. That's how we survive the snicker of laughter. Sometimes, even when we're surrounded, we feel all by ourselves in this world. But we're not.

Ignore that Call

"Stay away from ungodly babbling because it will only lead deeper into a godless lifestyle."1 Timothy 2:16 (VOICE)

The Holy Spirit abides in every Christian heart, and the uneasinesses I felt was a warning for me to evacuate that phone call. God is the protector our hearts, alerting us to falsities that attempt to crack through the surface.

What is*"ungodly babbling?"* Paul warned of false teachers, whose grand assumptions illuminated a lack of knowledge. In **1 Timothy 1:4**, he warns,*"Tell them to turn away from fables and endless genealogies. These activities just cause more arguments and confusion."*

Gossip operates on opinion. Faith is fueled by fact.

"Once these empty voices start to speak, Timothy, they infect and spread; and soon the body is consumed with its cancer." 2 Timothy 2:17 (VOICE)

The more we entertain gossip, the more likely we are to consider it. Aiming to operate in peace with someone by allowing them air out their opinion puts our hearts at risk for misaligned empathy. Yes, listen patiently to people, but draw a clear line of tolerance. [23]

Gossip is rooted in insecurity. Conversation that is focused on negative attributes and here-say is never worth the time it takes to entertain. We're not doing our friends any favors by entertaining it, and we need friends to call us out on it.

The Fringe

---

[23] "A Prayer for Those Caught in the gossip Trap," Meg Bucher

*"These are just the beginning of all that he does,
   merely a whisper of his power." Job 26:14a*

"Mom," my younger daughter asked, *"can you read these directions
to me?"*

No, don't think it's cute. Kid can read. It's not cute anymore …now,
it's laziness.

"You know how to read them," I point out, *"you just don't feel like
it."*

I heard the compliant seat-settling from the other end of the house,
and a mumbling sound of directions being read. She's right on the
fringe of being a super grown up kid …and she's not quite sure how
she feels about it. She still wants to need me, sometimes.

Job wrestled, knowing God could have ended His suffering in a
heartbeat if it would have been His omnipotent will to. Which he
also wrestled with …why was it God's will for Him to suffer? Why
was he allowed to suffer unjustly?

"Why won't you just read me the directions, mom?!" came an
entitled bark from a tiny desk chair.

"Because I believe you can, and it's time you do." I simply state.

There are times throughout Job's massive wrestle with suffering that
He was on the fringe of something …

**"If only there were someone to arbitrate between us, to lay his
hand upon us both, someone to remove God's rod from me, so that
his terror would fritter me no more. Then I would speak up without
fear of him, but as it now stands with me, I cannot." Job 9: 33-35**

On the fringe. But we know this side of the Gospel what Job was not privy to in Old Testament life.

Jesus.

How many times has God answered my *"can't you just do this"* prayer with *"I believe you can get through it, and it's time you do."*

We choose to walk in the maturity level of the wisdom we've been blessed with. Tempted to take the lazy route and laugh along or nod in agreement, we can instead push the conversational brake to re-route the conversation with: 'I disagree' or 'That's not kind.'

Friend Requests

Social Media is a breeding ground for broken friendship. We must set healthy boundaries and expectations for people that we meet and communicate with solely on social media. Great friendships can be formed and fostered there, but false and opportunistic friendships abound right alongside.

Scott Sauls addressed the challenges of social media on friendship in his book, Befriend. *"Partisans exaggerate the best features of their side and the worst features, real or contrived, or the opposing side. They minimize and overlook the weaknesses of their side, while dismissing the best features of the opposing side. What you end up with is someone being demonized and someone else being baptized by the crowds."*

The only way to guard our hearts against a virtual tear-down is to run to Christ in humility each day, studying His Word and staying His course for our lives. No one has the power to knock us off course unless we give it to them. Submit to God alone, and when we find a negative comment thread, don't read it. Vow to keep anything but what God says about us, out of our hearts. [24]

Let's Pray ...

Father,

Praise You for godly friends who hold us accountable. Thank You for illuminating the deceitful power of gossip, that we all entertain within earshot daily. We learned through the story of Job and his friends that misinformation can be just as damaging to our souls. We pray that Your voice is louder than all others. That we hear Your Word and Your Truth louder than any other voice or influence in our lives. Our character is compromised when we entertain lies.

We become enslaved by sin, and far from You. That's not what we want for our lives, Father. We want to reflect Your love and Your grace. Keep us in tune with Your will. And if what we see, hope for, or want does not align with Your will, replace it with what is. Help us to **"Stay away from ungodly babbling because it will only lead deeper into a godless lifestyle."1 Timothy 2:16 (VOICE)**

Forgive us for listening to it instead of walking away. We confess that often we don't speak up out of fear of rejection, and pray that you help us to have the courage to honor others with kind words when their character is being publicly slain.

Bless and heal those who have been mangled by gossip, and others enslaved by it's addictive habit. Heal our insecurities, and help us learn to turn to you for affirmation. Make us busy serving others in love to give You glory, instead of sitting in circles of babble and participating in chatter-filled phone calls. Empower us with Your

---

[24] "10 Types of Harmful Friends and How to Set Boundaries with Each," https://www.ibelieve.com/slideshows/10-harmful-types-of-friends-and-how-to-set-boundaries-with-each.html

Holy Spirit to heed Your warnings, and steer our conversations with Your love.

In Jesus' Name,
Amen. [25]

---

[25] "A Prayer for Those Stuck in the Gossip Trap," https://www.crosswalk.com/devotionals/your-daily-prayer/a-prayer-for-those-caught-in-the-gossip-trap-your-daily-prayer-january-19-2018.html

Chapter 13

"Friending"
Filtering Friendship on Social Media

"Do you have facebook?"

I hadn't see my college teammate and friend in years, but her laugh at the thought of anything that people-ly remained unchanged.

"Are you sure you didn't invent facebook?" she joked, as the *"I want to be friends with everyone"* joke lived on.

Friend-ing is a thing now, but it wasn't part of my generation's childhood. Now, there are many platforms available to make friends. Each with it's own distinct personality, style, etiquette, and vibe.

A stint in Social Media Marketing lent me an inside perspective to what is OK and not OK out on social media. Well, at least "back then." In the early 2000's …ancient …social media was just coming onto the scene. And it was really bad etiquette to self-promote. Advertising was unheard of. Now, people are capitalizing on social media, while those that sought to connect genuinely with people are fleeing for other outlets.

Is it possible to detect anything genuine on social media?
That's hard enough to unearth voice to voice or face-to-face.

The pro's and con's of social media can be hotly debated, but one thing is clear …the majority of us maintain some type of presence there. Even if just to keep up with T-ball practice or the PTO facebook page. Social media is woven into the way we communicate, and it's important for us to get a handle on it. The world will only continue to get smaller as we connect easier and easier with people from all corners of it.

In a meeting for a volunteer ministry I briefly served, there were people from no less than six countries on the same video conference call. That's amazing! God can literally put a worldwide team together in minutes. However, the downfall of being so easily connected is the risk we run of disengaging. Even "engagement" has become a coined term, which makes my stomach turn. Because in our striving, we will run to reach the mark but many miss the point.

There are two things that we have to filter our feeds through before opening the floodgates to world-wide friendship.

1. Jealousy
2. Comparison

Jealousy- resentment against a rival, a person enjoying success or advantage, etc., or against another's success or advantage itself.

Jealousy isn't a new thing that social media brought upon us. Hagar and Sarai illustrate a story of jealousy in the sixteenth chapter of the Bible.

"Now Sarai, Abrams wife, had borne him no children. But she had an Egyptian maidservant named Hagar; so she said to Abram, 'The Lord has kept me from having children. Go, sleep with my maidservant; perhaps I can build a family through her.'" Genesis 16:1-2 (NIV)

Right?! No set up for extreme jealousy there, or anything. Holy cow, jealousy!

"When she became pregnant, she began to despise her mistress. Then Sarai said to Abram, 'You are responsible for the wrong I am suffering. I put my servant in your arms, and now that she knows I'm pregnant, she despises me." Genesis 16:4b-5a NIV

I wonder if those outside of this dysfunctional circle viewed their situation the way we scroll through our news feeds. A new baby and a happy family. Just as our screens negate to communicate, on the inside, the household was in disarray. But the Lord saw Hagar.

"You are the God who sees me." Genesis 16:13a

He sees us. He sees everyone else. God sees behind the scrolling. Honestly, He's the only one that sees into the true depths of our hearts, social media or not.

"I have now seen the One who sees me." Genesis 16:13b

When we pray for the perspective to see people the way God sees them, we get a glimpse of what we cannot observe plainly. We can hit the like button and actually mean it. We can say that we'll pray for them and really write their name in our journal and on our hearts in prayer. Don't put it past God to use every channel of communication to connect us to each other ...and to Christ. Let's not allow our enemy to fuel our bent towards jealousy, but instead keep our perspective in check as we swipe.

Compare- to examine (two or more objects, ideas, people, etc.) in order to note similarities and differences.

Peninnah and Hannah knew comparison. Hannah could not bear children, Peninniah could, and they shared a husband. Hannah was poked and prodded and ridiculed by her rival, which is what stronger people do their seemingly weaker counterparts.

"And because the Lord had closed her womb, her rival kept provoking her in order to irritate her." 1 Samuel 1:6 NIV

How awful. I have unfollowed people to escape the pangs of comparison that stop me from being effective in what God has called me to do. Our perspective lack compared to another's proposed gain numbs the flow of our own blessings. Those people may not have done anything wrong. But what we see can fuel the mess inside of our own hearts.

"In bitterness of soul Hannah wept much and prayed to the Lord. And she made a vow, saying,

'O Lord Almighty, if you will only look upon your servant's misery and remember me, and not forget your servant but give her a son, then I will give him to the Lord for all the days of his life, and no razor will ever be used on his head."
1 Samuel 1:10-11 NIV

She poured out her soul to the Lord and He heard her. Her son was Samuel. When we are frustrated with our own lack, do we cry out to the Lord? Do we realize that we are allowed to ...rather, encouraged and welcome ...to talk to God frankly? He, who can illuminate what we cannot see and provide what we lack? Comparison and jealousy reflect our lack of trust in God.

These two filters will block the good that God calls us to see in every person He created. Social media is a highlight real. It's everyone's best foot forward. Or, everyone's rant against what they don't like about the world. When we recognize it for what it is, it allows compassion to flow and find a way to see God's purpose there. We begin to cheer each other on for the highlights that we've captured amidst what is promised to be a rough journey.

Let's be real, here …we don't walk out into the world wearing a sign that says, *"I had a blow-out fight with my husband last night."* Why would we post that on social media? Be honest. That's a phone call we make to a close and trusted friend. A cup of coffee we cry over with our Savior in search of answers. It's not what we air out on social media.

We can choose to scroll through social media through the lens of what we know. Our "friends" have human struggles and smiles they fight for. Make an internal commitment to cheer on those smiles they have fought to rally and post. Knowing that behind the happy profile picture, a world may be crumbling and a heart may ache. We recognize the facade because we all do it. And you know what? It's OK.

God tells us not to worry, to be joyful always, and to run the race. Flooding the feeds with positivity is a good thing. Choose not to follow the rants. When we go out into the world, we have a choice on what we filter in and out. Movies, TV shows, books we read … we have a choice as to what we see. Social media is the same. We can unfollow. And that's OK, too.

It got to me, too. The constant inundation of advertising and unattainable comparisons drove me into a season of distraction and discontent. My failure to fully engage in a conversation was frightening, and the time that I spent scrolling through feeds and updating statuses is embarrassing to admit!

Trying to be friends with everyone is overwhelming in a world where our technological ability to connect with each other produces a seemingly endless stream of new friends. But peace comes when we adopt God's perspective plan for friendship and connectedness over our limited ability to understand how He works all things for the greater good. [26]

Like anything in life, social media is something that we have to construct healthy boundaries for. The same Biblical truths we apply to our "real life" relationships can serve as solid guidelines regarding social media "friends."

The Pre-Scrolling Condition of Our Hearts.

"What we wear into our relationships will directly affect the health of those relationships ...healthy relationships begin with me, but they are not about me." -Pastor Todd Nielsen.

Pastor Todd's message on relationships resonated with this book on friendship I'd been working on at the time, and inspired me to pass some of the wisdom I absorbed onto my readers. *Colossians 3:12 states, "as God's chosen people, holy and dearly loved, clothe yourselves with compassion, kindness, humility, gentleness, and patience." (NIV)*

The VOICE paraphrase reads, *"Since you are set apart by God, made holy and dearly loved, clothe yourselves with a holy way of life: compassion, kindness, humility, gentleness, and patience."*

What is the pre-scrolling condition of our hearts? Before we let images and verbiage into our minds and hearts, what roots exist to translate it through the perspective of God's grace?

"God's chosen people..." We are chosen. He chose us. *"Set apart by God...."* We are set apart. God set us apart. Do we log on through a lens of a chosen and set apart child of the King to minister to His

---

[26] "10 Surprising Things I Learned after Quitting Social Media," https://www.ibelieve.com/slideshows/10-surprising-things-i-learned-after-quitting-social-media.html

people? We should. I believe that's the point. God's not unaware of what's happening on social media. In fact, He's weaving right through it.

Tenderhearted mercy is a holy way of life. *"The key to remain unified is to show compassion and forgiveness toward one another."* -*VOICE* commentary

To clothe ourselves with kindness takes more than action …it's attitude. *C.S. Lewis wrote that humility is thinking about ourselves less.* Wearing humility into our relationships serves others.

Gentleness is defined as: *kindly; amiable; not severe, rough or violent; mild.* It is moderation, gradualness, easily handled or managed; soft or low.

Patience is turning outward in consideration of what's going on around us, not our expectations of what others can do for us …like us …or comment positively about us…. Do we see the thread of opposition being stacked upon social media? The majority of what we witness out there is directly opposed to standards of kindness, humility, compassion, forgiveness, and gentleness.

Let's be honest …it's our gut reaction. That's how we all innately feel before we run our emotions through the filter of God's wisdom. We are incapable of producing the good fruit of His love by our own efforts. Logging on to social media is akin to walking out into the world. Seeking God's wisdom before we walk to into the world will be evident. Preparation begins long before we start hitting the like button and filling in the comment fields. It starts with a daily pursuit of Christ's calling on our lives.

Authentic faith shines through all platforms. When we're willing to share our lives on social media, we are allowing God to minister His comfort and hope through them. He's can use what we've got …

right now. We're not called to fight blind, but equipped ...for every good work. I believe that includes social media.

The Responsibility Linked to the Power of the Click.

"In your relationships, you have great power ...great strength ...We can use it to crush people, or care for people." -Pastor Todd Nielsen

Colossians 2:13 says, "Put up with one another. Forgive. Pardon any offenses against one another, as the Lord pardoned you, because you should act in kind." (VOICE)

The NIV version states, *"Bear with each other and forgive one another if any of you has a grievance against someone. Forgive as the Lord forgave you."*

Forgiving others because the Lord forgave us is not to make us take the stance of a perpetual doormat. It's *"Freeing the other person from the guilt for what they've done." -Pastor Todd Nielsen.* We are so reactionary out there on social media. React. React. React.

We may spend three days praying about an increased time commitment, but react immediately when we've been attacked on social media. When we let our gut reactive words out without checking them, if often exposes our internal struggles. Things like jealousy and comparison can sneak into the back of our minds and derail our lives.

Think Before Responding

One of the biggest challenges posed by social media is the temptation to wage and win comment wars. Some are started by trollers, whose sole purpose is to stir up conflict. When we scroll upon a discussion we are tempted to dive into, it's best to walk away from the device. If, after a substantial length of time (personally, I wait at least an entire day) there is still a desire to respond, than do so with grace and wisdom. We're called to seek peace through our words, even when an assertive response is warranted.

When we stumble upon some crushing criticism from someone we've *"friend-ed"* on social media, it tests our tendency to react. We can choose not to be offended. Refuse to be disqualified for what God has qualified and called us to do. Especially by people that exist in our lives solely on social media.

We can all choose to look an unfair misunderstanding of our character as the test that it is, and a part of the imperfect shreds of humanity that bind us. It hurts to be hurt by someone we may have admired from a distance, but we can't give it the power to derail the mission God has set forth in our lives.

There is a clip that stands out in my mind in the depths of all the books and podcasts I've digested. *From every leader, we will learn what kind of leader we want to be ...and what kind of leader we don't want to be.*

We can choose to move forward from character attacks with a heart of grace, and lessons learned. Lessons that will continue to grow us as people, when we chose to turn a hurtful slam into a beautiful step closer to our Savior. This kind of forgiveness is hard, but it's possible when we listen to God's voice above all others. It also helps us to create some healthy boundaries moving forward. And we must keep moving forward.

Bitterness will threaten to take root when we're unfairly attacked, and comparison and disqualification crouch low at the starting line ...just waiting for the gun to go off. In the middle of a personal social media storm in my own life, I remembered an encouraging voice ... *"Father, give Meg the courage not to be perfect."*

Turning up the volume on encouraging words from people who actually know us in everyday life heals. That's how we survive social media with our heads still attached. The most important voice in that circle should be Christ. He will meet us in those moments to encourage and sharpen us.

It's important to take stock in how our comments represent our hearts. Word are powerful. Jesus held His ground, based in God's Truth. He is the Word. But He was never unjustly cruel or unkind in the way He executed His point. It's not in His character, and it shouldn't be in ours.

Love is the Point of it All.

"And over all these virtues put on love, which binds them all together in perfect unity." Colossians 3:14 (NIV)

The VOICE paraphrase states, *"But above all these, put on love! Love is the perfect tie to bind these together."*

Love and obedience are tied directly together.

John 15:10, "If you obey my commands, you will remain in my love, just as I have obeyed my Fathers' commands and remain in his love."

"Friend-ing," is not as much about us as we think. All friendships are meant to serve and glorify Him. When we filter with godly wisdom as we scroll, it lends us the opportunity to minster to the world.

If we wouldn't say it out loud in crowd or directly to someone's face, we probably shouldn't post it online. I firmly believe that Jesus can defend Himself. He's not worried about being attacked on social media. But I do believe He's concerned with how we're reacting. There's a saying, *"You'll never argue someone to faith."* But I do believe that we can love others right to His feet. By the way we live our lives and treat each other, we can reach out and into lives with the love of Christ.

Yes, on social media. Yes, in the land of the fake. Yes, in the land of the highlight reel. Yes, in the mine field where everyone is out to make a buck and everyone else is trying to control what we see …

Our God is bigger.
He sits above all.
Christ is in control.
He is aware …protecting us …and going before and behind us.
His voice created all.
God knew us when we were in our mother's womb.
He knows how our last hour will shake out.
God blesses us and purposes us.

He's bigger than social media.
He's placed us there purposefully.
Our charge is to use seconds spent scrolling wisely.

Christ set the example for us.
"Follow My example in obeying the Father's commandments and receiving His love. If you obey My commandments, you will stay in My love." John 15:10 (VOICE)

We are all capable of compassion. Love comes first. Christ demands it.

God calls us to light up the dark. We travel to dangerous corners of the globe to minister to the oppressed and spread the Gospel to those who have yet to hear it. Social media is not always safe …especially for our kids. One day over coffee, a friend shared concerns about a new social media channel our kids were crazy over, and her very legitimate fears on what they would see and who might see them. Our kids are elementary aged, and I explained that I had been letting them play around with the app on my device, but not unsupervised.

"It's actually a lot fun," I mused as I opened the app on my phone. Bracing ourselves as we scrolled through the feed, we saw a video a tween girl had posted of her recent baptism.

"What a witness," we both conquered. A light in the dark. Authentic, brave, and risky.

We have a Light that has already conquered the darkness. (John 10:10) He's for us. Who can be against us? Let's link arms to reach hearts hurting in the dark corners of the world. Some of them are now just a click away from the healing hope of Christ.

Let's Pray ...

Father,

Praise You for the life of Jesus and the lessons of Your Word. Thank You for the people that You place in our lives to sharpen us, and help us to forgive those who cut us down. We lift every shred of hate in our hearts, our line of sight, and our communities, to You in prayer. Grant us hearts full of His compassion and love for each other, as You command.

*Praise You, for **"You are the God who sees me." Genesis 16:13a** You remember us and see us and are there for us in a way that goes so far beyond how we know and understand the word, 'love.' We learned through the story of Hannah and Penniniah that Your way is higher, just, and full of the incomprehensible love that You shower upon us.*

*Social media is not out of Your line of sight. As we navigate the news feeds that invade our line of sight, You are there. It's a war online, as it is in the world. But we can minister to each other in that place. You promise that where we are gathered You will be there with us. It's important to guard our hearts and minds, and we pray Your will over our news feeds and those we choose to "follow." **The only One*** *we should truly be following is You. Help us to eliminate anything from our line of sight that could possibly invade, attack, and derail our walk with You. We can still be light on social media ...we can still spread the hope and love of the gospel, without risking the status of our own souls. Help us to understand and accept the risk of loving people for You, Father. Just as we go into dangerous places in the world and into the heart of our cities and jails to love on people ... help us to accept the risk of loving people extravagantly online and on social media. Help us get more feet into physical churches, that start from loving relationships in our lives ...both face to face and online.*

Colossians 3:12 states, "as God's chosen people, holy and dearly loved, clothe yourselves with compassion, kindness, humility, gentleness, and patience." *(NIV) Help us to maintain an accurate portrayal of our lives, and Your grace alive and active in it, both online and in person. Let the failures shine as bright as the blessings, because we know that even through the mistakes and missteps You are there, growing us and helping us.*

Colossians 2:13 says, "Put up with one another. Forgive. Pardon any offenses against one another, as the Lord pardoned you, because you should act in kind." *(VOICE) Lord, God, help us to choose not to be offended, and not to react in bitterness and argumentation to every little thing we disagree with or don't like, both online and in person. We are sent to be the peacekeepers. That doesn't mean we have to be doormats, but help us to cover everything we do and say with Your love. Because love is the point of it all.* **"And over all these virtues put on love, which binds them all together in perfect unity."** *Colossians 3:14 (NIV)*

Lord, You say, **"Follow My example in obeying the Father's commandments and receiving His love. If you obey My commandments, you will stay in My love."** *John 15:10 (VOICE)*

Help us to remember *John 10:10. "The thief comes only to steal and kill and destroy; I have come that they may have life, and have it to the full." (NIV)* For it is through the strength of Christ that we will find joy and peace.

In Jesus' Name,
Amen.

Chapter 14

Bullies.
What is it? How do we spot it? Can we stop it?

Bullies. We often talk about bullying in regards to our children. After-school special scenes of kids smashed into lockers, given wedgies or swirlies, or being laughed at by a pack of classmates. Now, cyber-bullying drives many tweens and teens into depression and to consider suicide. Young children often pick up behaviors that they see from the adults in their lives. And the adults in their lives might be the very bullies that smashed someone into a locker, gave out wedgies and swirlies, cackled in a pack at a classmate's expense, or cyber-bullied someone right out of school.

Adulthood is not immune to bullies. Not everyone outgrows bullying behavior. *"Bullies are made, not born, and it happens at an early age, if the normal aggression of 2-year-olds isn't handled well."*[27]

Who are they?

It's hard to find loyal friends. Our innate need for companionship sometimes leads us to tolerate bad friendship in fear of the loneliness we might experience without them. Letting our guard down with the wrong person is just as dangerous to our souls as trusting no one.

---

[27] https://www.psychologytoday.com/us/basics/bullying

This chapter will address the importance of instilling God-led boundaries in our lives, and how to recognize and reconcile with bullying.

bully- a blustering, quarrelsome, overbearing person who habitually badgers and intimidates smaller or weaker people. (dictionary.com)

Other definitions of the word include verbiage like, *"loudly arrogant."*
The Bible is full of examples of people *not* to emulate right alongside the hall of heroes and redemptive stories. We have to guard our hearts in assurance that we don't get lost or detoured by following the wrong persona.

Psychology Today defines bullying as *"a distinctive pattern of harming and humiliating others, specifically those who are in some way smaller, weaker, younger or in any way more vulnerable than the bully."*

Always forgive, but choose wisely. In adulthood, it can be hard to avoid getting caught up with an overbearing bully. Especially when we've just moved to a new town or started a new chapter in life. Turn the page cautiously. We're called to love our neighbor. The best way to befriend a bully is to be kind at an arm's length.

Common Characteristics of Grown Bullies

False Flattery

Bullies are carelessly careful with their words. Their comments can creep in through the back door of our psyche. **They quickly become masters at making insults sound like complements.** Beware of people that follow every insult and sarcastic dig at someone else's character with a *"God love him/her"* or a *"you know I'm just* *kidding,"* as if it's a magic eraser for each rude remark. Beware of the slippery slope of false flattery. It's a big sign of the early stages of manipulation ...aka ...bullying.

"He who rebukes a man will in the end gain more favor than he who has a flattering tongue." Proverbs 28:23 NIV

Entertaining their comments bodes us more likely to begin considering them. Bullies tend to gravitate towards fearful or-self-conscious people who have trouble being assertive enough to call them out on their nasty tongues.

<u>Overly Critical</u>

Bullying is characterized by overly critical comments that humiliate one considered lesser than they. It also surfaces in everyday conversations as advice on how to handle parts of our lives that we never asked their opinion of. These people seek control, and have a very high opinion of themselves. A bully assumes the purpose of every conversation is for them to tell whomever they are talking to what they should be doing.

1 Corinthians 15:33 NIV states,
"Do not be misled: 'Bad company corrupts good character.'"

The slope from entertaining their advice to actually implementing it in our lives is slippery! Be careful to duck out of overbearing conversations. It's OK to be assertive enough to say, *"I wasn't asking for your advice, I just needed a friend to listen."* Or to answer a sarcastic insult with, *"That wasn't funny at all."*

Be ready for a possible kick-back, accused of over-sensitivity, or blown off when the bully can't have their way. Remember 1 Corinthians 15:33, and don't be afraid to stand firmly convicted with kindness and grace. Let compassion for the pain those who aim to hurt others must endure drive fear away from an assertive stand on what's righteous.

They Don't Listen

Those that bully others are often not good listeners. We may be assertive enough to shut down sarcastic digs on our personalities and unwanted advice, but don't be surprised if their behavior doesn't change. They may not have heard you. This is especially hard when friends reveal themselves as bullies.

"Wounds from a sincere friend are better than many kisses from an enemy." Proverbs 27:6 (NLT)

Before I learned all I know today about boundaries and assertiveness, I once gave a friend seven years to hear me. Bullies will act as if everything they put us through happened in our imagination, or by the fault of our own misunderstanding or sensitivity. Somehow, my earnest attempt to communicate my hurt over the years were never catalogued in with all of our other conversations. This led to shock at my eventual pulling away from that friendship.

On the cusp of forty as I write this book, I have learned to seek genuine and sincere friendships in my life. Authentic friendships are rooted in honesty, even when butting heads. Honesty builds layers of trust into our friendships, so they aren't de-railed over every little misunderstanding. Learning to listen to our fiends is important. Chose to keep company with friends who lend an honest ear, and move boldly away from those that do not.

When our words fall on deaf ears, remember that only God can change hearts.

They Don't Seem Like Bullies

A pre-school friend of my daughter's used to push my younger daughter around. By the time my four year old figured out how to tell me something was making her uncomfortable when they played alone, I had already started to notice a change in her little sister. It took extensive effort on my part to interrupt the way she was processing what she witnessed. I could read the story of what had happened to her by the change in her behavior. Suddenly hitting another child, snapping a quick mean remark, or asking others to "please leave."

My toddler outgrew the behavior with our help, but that same *"friend"* went on to bully my daughter, and many of her classmates.

Some kids are masters at putting on a nice face in front of adults. Beware of the adults with an *overly nice* facade. They can pack a punch as mean as the stand-offish or outspoken bully. Nothing may seem wrong on the surface. They may even be able to convince you that it's just kids being kids, or that their occasional slip in behavior is because no one is perfect.

"At some level, we naturally love ourselves; but it's not natural to love others well, especially those who have wronged or wounded us in some way." DeMoss Wolgemuth

As children of God we are forgiving and accepting people. But it's OK to call a spade a spade, and move out of the line of fire. God never intended for us to resume doormat status. They may have always been that way, and though we can certainly lead them in a different directions, it's not our lot in life to change them.

"Bullying is not garden-variety aggression; it is a deliberate and repeated attempt to cause harm to others of lesser power. It's a very durable behavioral style, largely because bullies get what they want- at least at first." [28]

28 https://www.psychologytoday.com/us/basics/bullying

God blessed us with good instincts. If something feels off, take it to Him. Seek His wisdom. He is faithful to help us guard our hearts. Bullies can be like chameleons, changing with each passing crowd and situation. Wait for friends who are consistent and dependable, no matter the situation.

"Do not let any unwholesome talk come out of your mouths, but only what is helpful for building others up according to their needs, that it may benefit those who listen. And do not grieve the Holy Spirit of God, with whom you were sealed for the day of redemption. Get rid of all bitterness, rage and anger, brawling and slander, along with every form of malice. Be kind and compassionate to one another, forgiving each other, just as in Christ God forgave you." Ephesians 4:29-32

There are more characteristics of bullying, and I encourage anyone who feels bullied to bravely research the behavior that they are enduring. (If someone is physically hurting you, remove yourself from that situation immediately.)Prayerfully search Scripture for wisdom, and expect that God will faithfully speak into your situation. Patience, prayer, and humility will allow us to traverse sticky situations with grace and love.

Biblical Bullying?

Could that be possible? The Bible is full of things that we still have to deal with in modern day life. Despite the vast cultural difference, human beings still struggle with many of the same things that ancient people did.

Pharaoh

In Genesis Chapter 40, Pharaoh puts two of his officials in prison. "Pharaoh was angry with his two officials," (v.2) is the only explanation provided. What did the cupbearer do? Hold his cup wrong? Let a grape-seed drift to the bottom of the cup? And how about the chief baker?

The NIV Cultural Backgrounds Study Guide gives us a clearer picture of their responsibilities. *"The potential for assassination attempts through the king's food and drink was real and constant, so these officials not only needed to be incorruptible themselves, but also had to be able to hire people above reproach and identify attempts at infiltration of the staff by enemies of the king. The text is silent concerning their offense, but since both were responsible for meals it seems logical to speculate that the king may have gotten sick from a meal."*

These two men had important relationships with Pharaoh. Probably, dare I assume, the closest thing he might have had to friends ...in order to trust them with what he ate amidst assassination attempts. Yet they are thrown in jail. One is eventually restored, but the other is beheaded. We aren't made privy to Pharaoh's logic in this decision, but both scenarios do fulfill Joseph's interpretation of their dreams while in jail.

"Do not make friends with a hot-tempered man, do not associate with one easily angered, or you may learn his way and get yourself ensnared." Proverbs 22:23-24 (NIV)

Ahithophel

Ahithophel was a wise counselor, and *2 Samuel 16:23 tells us how he befriended David. "Now in those days the advice Ahithopel gave was like that of one who inquires of God. That was how both David and Absalom regarded all of Ahithopel's advice."* The NIV Study Bible Notes tell us that he was Bathsheba's grandfather, who "secretly aligned himself against David for his treatment of Bathsheba and Uriah." Listen to David's angst over the "unsuspected betrayal by a trusted friend." (NIV Study Bible Notes.)

"Even my close friend, someone I trusted, one who shared my bread, has turned against me." Psalm 41:9 (NIV)

Shattered friendships are victims of this broken world. We aren't going to be able to detect, prevent, and mend every friendship or hurt. We must be so careful when extending deep friendship, a vast allocation of time, and an open heart, not to be manipulated. This is where healthy boundaries play a very important role. "I can't believe I said/did that" moments sometimes stem from slips in judgement and failure to enforce our boundaries.

David had made some heavy mistakes that Ahithophel could not shake. The treatment of Bathsheba, and the murder of Uriah. We endure much less heavy circumstances of betrayal that still scar us to the core. That's when forgiveness seems like scaling a mountain, and reconciliation often fades from view. Had we constructed and stuck to some good boundaries, we might have had the opportunity to sharpen one another rather than repeat a lesson we had already learned.

"If an enemy were insulting me, I could endure it; if a foe were rising against me, I could hide. But it is you, a man like myself, my companion, my close friend, with whom I once enjoyed sweet fellowship at the house of God, as we walked about among the worshipers." Psalm 55:12-14 (NIV)

Betrayal will tear a friendship down. And what for this betrayal of David's friendship? Though he would live out the dire consequences of his actions towards Bathsheeba and Uriah, God did not leave David. See, God is the ultimate judge. **When we start to harbor our own system of justice, the relationship is destined to derail.**

"When Ahithophel saw that his advice had not been followed, he saddled his donkey and set out for his house in his hometown. He put his house in order and then hanged himself. So he died and was buried in his father's tomb." 2 Samuel 17:23 (NIV)

In fear that he would be found and charged with treason as the rebellion failed, he panicked and ended his life. He couldn't see a solution. And moreover, He couldn't trust God for it. When we fail to trust our friendships to God's just hands, they come unwound. We are simply not built to make the final judgement on another's character, or our own. God alone, writes the end of our stories.

Judas

Judas' life ended in the same fashion as Ahithophel. Out of manipulative moves. Lost and panicked because he missed what Jesus had cut him in on all those days he walked in his inner circle of followers. Or perhaps it was Jesus' words ringing in his ears, *"woe to that man who betrays the Son of Man! It would be better for him if he had not been born." (Matthew 26:24 NIV)* We do this, don't we? Confuse death and consequences? Thinking that the consequences of our bad choices, however painful to live out, will somehow overshadow Grace?

The pressure of the crowd got to Judas. *"What are you willing to give me if I hand him over to you?" (Matthew 26:15 NIV)* What's in it for me? *"Judas, are you betraying the Son of Man with a kiss?" Luke 22:48 NIV* This crowd of prominent stature, *"chief priests, the officers of the temple guard, and the elders" (Luke 22 52 NIV)* lured Judas into thinking that it would somehow benefit him more to betray than obey the Son of Man.

Before we are too hard on Judas, we can jump just a few verses forward to find Peter caving in to similar pressure from the crowd. *"Then seizing him, THEY led him away and took him into the house of the high priest. Peter followed at a distance. But when THEY had kindled a fire in the middle of the courtyard and had sat down together, Peter sat down with THEM." Luke 22: 54-56 NIV, emphasis mine.*

Peter shortly thereafter denied Jesus three times, as predicted. He eventually came back to Jesus. Judas fled in shame. Peter got it enough to know that the love of Jesus was bigger than anything he couldn't work out and all the things he messed up and misspoke. Judas gave up.

There are friends who simply give up and run for the hills, leaving us to wonder why and pick up the pieces. But when the sting of betrayal lingers, it's crucial to understand that in the grand scheme of life, the devil intends on deceitfully dropping bombs into our friendships.

Forgive forward. Have compassion. Even if reconciliation seems impossible. In an imperfect world, guarding our hearts sometimes means walking away so that God can move. We may not always understand, and it may not always be our fault. But we are all working through this broken world in an imperfect way. Messes, fallouts, betrayal, and broken trust are bound to fall upon us.

Cultivating Kindness

Bullying is an epidemic, and it's not limited to physical harm. Mental torment can lead grown adults to question the very core of their self worth.

The heartbreaking truth about bullying is that the bullies aren't always aware of the damage they are causing, and we're not always brave enough to tell them. We shrink back in fear, and by doing so rob them of the opportunity to repent and see the error of their ways.

The mental strain an emotionally bullying relationship puts on the human heart can be devastating, because sometimes it can look ...

and even feel …like friendship and acceptance. By the time we're wise to what's going on, it can be extremely hard to back away. [29]

When we are in toxic situations, prayer is the most powerful weapon to help us pull out and away. The Bible tells us to be honest with each other. It's especially important to tell people close to us when they've hurt us, and it's important to understand what God says about when to walk away.

Be Kind to Yourself

Enduring adult relationships requires us to first be kind to ourselves. Reminding ourselves who God says we are lofts His voice above all snarky and manipulative tones. In fact, spending time with Him daily will help us become wise to mean behavior.

Nancy DeMoss Wolgemuth wrote, in her book *"Lies Women Believe and The Truth that Sets them Free:"*

"According to God's Word, if you are a child of God, the Truth is:
*You are created in the image of God. (Gen 1:27)
*He loves you, and you are precious to Him. (Eph. 2:4, 1 John 3:1)"

To cultivate kindness in the wake of bullying, or in any situation we find ourselves in throughout life, we must choose to believe who and Whose we are. If we can embrace that truth, it unlocks our potential to walk out our purpose in everyday life. Our purpose is to love others. Even the bullies. Frankly, especially the bullies. They obviously suffer from believing a few lies.

Whenever I get knicked up training for a race, I visit the local health store. They specialize in helping others find a natural way to help

---

[29] "How to Protect Your Family from Bullying,"https://www.crosswalk.com/family/parenting/kids/how-to-protect-your-family-from-bullying.html

their bodies heal not only from the outside, but the inside. I often feel fit on the outside, but I'm not always healthy on the inside. Injury often signals a larger deficit.

"You have to be kind to yourself!" my friend reminded.

She's right! We cannot expect our bodies to perform at maximum capacity if we're robbing them of the nutrients they need to fuel us.

Friendships carry the same warning signs. An imploding friendship is seldom one person's fault. For most of my life, I have struggled with assertiveness and boundaries. When I began to recognize and address those areas of weakness in my own life, my friendships became more honest and authentic. I am now a better friend to others. Imagine my progress had I just blamed others for smothering me instead of learning how to construct healthy boundaries?!

"As we believe and receive God's love, we can be set free from self-loathing, comparison, and self-absorption. And then we can become channels through home His love can flow out to others." -Lies Women Believe

Love truly is the key, even to bullying. God grows us through every situation. Taking an assertive stand not to tolerate bad behavior from a friend takes brave grace, but it's worth it. True friendship is rooted in honesty, and good friends will care that you've been hurt by their misspoken words. How can we get rid of bullying if those that are bullying are unaware of their behavior?

Learn to Love

Scripture gives us many examples of loyal friends within imperfect friendships. Abram was a loyal friend to Lot, even after their land dispute and separation.

"When Abram heard that his relative had been taken captive, he called out the 318 trained men born in his household and went in pursuit as far as Dan. During the night Abram divided his men to attack them and he routed them, pursing them as far as Hobah, north of Damascus. He recovered all the goods and brought back his relative Lot and his possessions, together with the women and the other people." Genesis 14:14-16 (NIV)

Love requires obedience. Jesus linked love to obedience over and over again, calling the true sentiments of our hearts to take action. He also commands us to love our enemy. Anyone that has ever felt adversity come against them knows that loving an enemy is done out of an obedient heart.

"My command is this: Love each other as I have loved you." John 15:12

Compassion ... to forgive, pray for, and love our enemies. We must obediently focus our thoughts and behaviors on answering hate with compassion and love. Scripture tells us to *"take captive of every thought."*

Let us consider our Shepard and how He cares for His sheep, seeking not one to be lost. Can we encourage each other without assuming and assigning motives? Jesus doesn't treat us like that. He loves us for who we are, and meets us where we are at. Right or wrong, He loves us, and He calls ALL of us to follow His lead. [30]

We've most likely been on both sides of the spectrum. We're all learning how to navigate relationships and put up God-led boundaries. It's a process that we will never perfect. We all have words we wish we could take back, and situations that we would replay differently. God's purpose for friendship is to minister to that

---

[30] "When You Can't Handle the Hate," https://www.crosswalk.com/faith/spiritual-life/when-you-can-t-handle-the-hate.html

process. Through the hurts and triumphs we endure with each other, we can move closer to Him.

Let's Pray,

Father,
We praise You for each life, crafted differently by Your creative hand. Everyone carries a piece of Your purpose in their heart. Face outward, we have the opportunity to learn of the depth of Your love, and grow closer to You.

Father, we confess that there are times that we don't know how to take our emotion out of the picture in order to react correctly and compassionately. When bullied, we become defensive and bitter. It's easy to fall prey to vengeful thinking and to hurl insults back at the ones causing our pain. Forgive us for reacting in spite and blame. The bullies in life are Yours, too. You created them and You love them just as much as You love us and our children. Forgive us for forgetting that.

Help us to do what is not within our normal inclination. Through Your Spirit who dwells within us from the moment we believe in Jesus, give us the strength to be compassionate and kind in unjust situations. Focus our gaze on Your Son, and the sacrifice He chose to make for us.

Jesus understands what it's like to be bullied. Questioned and ridiculed for who He was His entire walk on this earth, and beaten to death in the most brutal way possible. By His death on the cross, He endured more physical and emotional pain than we will ever be asked to bear by our loving God. Christ took on the weight of the entire world's sin. By name, He knew us. By name, He forgave us ... long before we breathed earthly air.

*Jesus died for the bully and the bullied. He left us instructions to pray for our enemies. Just as He did in His last breath on the cross. **"Father, forgive them ...for they know not what they do."***

Father, Praise You for friendships and relationships, and for Your plan and purpose for each one. Jesus modeled friendship perfectly, but we seem to get it wrong a lot. Help us weave through our sinfully fallen society in attempt to be the open arms of love that we are called to be without having our souls trampled on.

We want our friendships to reflect Your purpose and plan, and to serve and glorify You. Allow us to see the relationships in our lives with Your perspective, Lord. Teach us to construct healthy and God-led boundaries.

Father, it's hard to see others hurt. Guide us to act swiftly in their defense and compassionately remind them of who they really are when their soul's are under attack.

Sometimes, the very definition of friendship is confused by bullying. When we are hurt by our very own friends, help us to seek Your counsel and guidance as we lead them in forming godly friendships. Bless our friendships to honor You, and help us to be loving and loyal friends to others.

Bless and protect our hearts and minds. By the power of the Holy Spirit who helps us to recall Your Word, may we have Truth on the tips of our tongues to remember what You say about us. May we always know that You love us, and that we are Yours. Stir our hearts to hear Your call on our lives, and may our steps follow fast after You all of our days.

Help us to remember to pray for our enemies. To pray for the bullies. Bless those that harbor malice and anger in their hearts, treating others as less than what they are ...Your beautiful creation. Search their hearts for hurt and call them back to You. Love their hurt away.

Help us, Jesus. Beyond our mistakes and inabilities, bless our feet to walk out our calling, and to hear Your voice above all others ...

In Jesus' Name,
Amen.

Conclusion

To my new-found friends …

As Christians, we are called to be friends with everyone. God's definition of friendship doesn't mean tolerating everyone all at once, or reaching out to fill everyone else's needs all at once. From His perspective, we are to be flipped outward in service to love others. Ready and willing to befriend anyone He places in our paths, by His standards. Boundaries protect us from pride. Sometimes the best way to be a friend to someone is to say, *"No, I love you but I can't go there with you."*

Love people. Love friends. Be encouraged by the process that it is, and embrace the beautifully imperfect people we are. We were not meant to go through this life alone, and all need a supportive group of people to surround and encourage us. I hope that through our journey, you feel one step closer to God …and each other.

"Be joyful always."
1 Thessalonians 5:16

If we're open to His wisdom, joy will come. Not fleeting happiness, but joy. Friends that will weave in and out of our lives, friends we may never meet face-to-face, friends that stick like family, and friends that are family. Find God first, and friendship will follow. It's not so much about us, but everything about what He plans to do through us.

Happy Friending!
Megs

To my friends ...

Friendship is my favorite.

I love my friends. Many days, I looked through a screen of tears as I typed, remembering all the laughter we have shared over the years. From big city suburb to small lake town, my life has been surrounded by so many outstanding people. You are all a part of this book. Childhood friends, High School and College Teammates, Sorority sisters, all of the old boat friends, neighborhood friends, 'Mom" friends, Bible Study girls, our dance family, coaches and pastors. These are the people that recognize my laugh before they see my face. Thank you for building me up, picking me up, and cheering me on. For disagreeing with me and calling me out when I needed to hear it. God has loved me so much through all of you. Thank you is insufficient. I'm forever grateful. To the few I hold closest to my heart ...

"Five Alive,"
I was blessed with an amazing family. Parents who have been married almost 40 years as a write this, and an amazing brother and sister. It's not easy to be the oldest child, and our family is far from perfect, but those first friendships laid the groundwork for who I am today and how I treat other people. Not everyone is blessed with a good and godly example to follow, but we were. And wow, am I ever thankful.

Gram - I miss you everyday. Your friendship was probably the most important in my life. One that has continued to grow even after you left for heaven. The notes you left behind, the wisdom and stories you shared, and the memories we made, linger like no time has passed. It's hard to find someone willing to listen to all that a young girl has to say, but you always did. I loved our conversations. Thank you for instilling a faith in Jesus in me, and showing me how to love people like He does. I can still hear you singing church hymns and Sinatra. I can't wait to hug you and take a walk with you in heaven. I love you, Gram.

Dad, thank you for making sure I never went to sleep without knowing how much you loved me. Thank you for writing on comic strips and leaving them for me to find when you had to work odd shifts. No matter how many times I slammed the door, you faithfully put it back on it's hinges. I value every bit of wisdom you share with me ...whether it's what I want to hear or not. I love talking to you, Dad. Thank you for making me laugh and teaching me how to seek peace and love others for who they are.

*Mom, I'm not sure you realize what a beautiful person you are. I know it's not easy for you to find the words to say how you feel, but thank you for finding them in every card that you send me or note that I have saved. You raised me to be grateful and generous ...and when I am struggling you remind me who I am. Thank you, Mom, for teaching me to be a strong and determined woman. You **are** beautiful. I love you.*

Excited understates how it felt to welcome you into the world, little sis. Colleen, I know I have literally smothered you with love over the years, but I'm not sorry. Having a sister was a dream come true for me. It's true, there's no friendship quite like sisterhood. It's a joy to share so many of your first memories as a mom with you as you did with me. No matter how many ways we're different, we're sill the same sisters. I'll always love you the same and believe in you, beautiful and incredibly talented Kin.

Cleveland sports fans share a bond, especially the CLE natives who have witnessed all the heartbreak that led up to the victory parade. But thank God for it all, because it's the bond that led my little brother and I out of sibling rivalry and into friendship. Michael, I respect the sacrifice and service you give to our country, and many ways you dedicate yourself selflessly to your family. Our conversations are always honest ...and hilarious. Love you, little bro. May the force be with you.

To the friend waiting in heaven already, I hope you're laughing at all the ridiculous moments with me just as loudly up there as you always did down here. I miss you so much, Christina. You made high school bearable for a girl that was almost too scared to move that first day. God put us in the same homeroom, the same neighborhood, in the same church row to worship on Sundays. You were always running late ...I can't believe you got there first!

Teammates often become close friends, but Kate, our friendship means more to me than most. Elenor Roosevelt said "Great minds discuss ideas, average minds discuss events; small minds discuss people." We laugh a lot, and that's my favorite. But, wow, do we discuss a lot of ideas, Kate. Without your friendship, my faith in Christ would not be what it is today. Love you, my friend!

To the friends with who have forgiven my mistakes and missteps, I hope one day we can see each other the way God sees us, regardless of past hurt we have caused each other. For the roads of forgiveness that did not lead to reconciliation have taught me the most about how to be a good friend. Thank you for the boundaries and the honesty that forced me to face my shortcomings, and seek His refinement in the process of life on earth.

About the Author

Meg is passionate about people, and the purposeful way we've been God-placed. She writes about everyday life within the love of Christ on her blog, Sunny&80. **https://sunnyand80.org.**

When she left the business world to be a stay-at-home mom, Sunny&80 became a way to retain the funny life-lessons God revealed through motherhood. Over time that small step of obedience led to freelance writing and Bible study leading. She's written two children's books, "The Hot Pink Dinosaur," and "The Purple Sparkly Unicorn."

Born and raised in a suburb of Cleveland, OH, Meg now lives in a nearby lake town with her husband, two daughters, and their Golden-doodle. Her family plays an active role in serving their local church. Her hobbies are running, photography, and anything outside and adventurous. Check out her daily pics on Instagram @sunnyandeighy. And ...Go Browns!

Made in the USA
Monee, IL
25 September 2019